A Shell Guide

SURREY

Bruce Watkin

A Shell Guide

SURREY

by Bruce Watkin

Faber & Faber 3 Queen Square London

First published in 1977
by Faber and Faber Limited
3 Queen Square London WC1
Printed in Great Britain by
Butler & Tanner Ltd, Frome and London
All rights reserved

ISBN 0 571 09609 3

Illustrations

Note: Captions to the photographs include place names in **bold type**. These refer to entries in the gazetteer, pages 37–189

Introduction

Surrey is small, hilly, agriculturally middling and within easy reach of London. It is populous and prosperous as well as deceptively rural. It lost large parts to London in 1880 and in 1955, and it was a small county already. It has only become populous since the end of the eighteenth century, and "within easy reach" since the middle of the nineteenth. Once it was the poorest and most sparsely populated of the home counties, with small settlements in the river valleys and a dribble along the northern fringe of the North Downs. There

◁ Near **Shere**
Cobbett Hill, **Normandy**
Reigate Heath
▽ From Castle Hill, **Bletchingley**

was little overspill from the city till much later, beyond the London bridgehead at Southwark.

It was favoured by royalty from Norman times for hunting, and from the seventeenth century for racing: hence the growth of Richmond and Kew, then Epsom and Ewell. (The palace of Nonsuch was at Ewell.) In fact, royal favour, the varied scenery, and an absence of agricultural competition gave rise to landscape improvement and outdoor activity on an unprecedented scale: racing, cricket, golf, gardening, walking, cycling and early motoring (Brooklands and the Brighton Run). These are virtues the county is proud of.

Long Wood, **Chipstead**

Near **Wotton** ▷

Epsom Downs

Physically, Surrey is a badly cut, many-layered, sandwich. The centre is a wedge of hardish chalk; the outsides are wedges of heavy clay. Within the latter are the smaller areas of barren Bagshot sands of NW Surrey and the long wedge of Greensand in southern Surrey. All tilt gently down to the north and have been worn away in proportion to their resistance so that the southern end of the chalk forms the North Downs scarp and the harder sandy beds stand out in bastions as at St George's Hill in the north, and Hindhead and Leith Hill in the south.

These sandy bastions were important in the Iron Age for isolated fortified settlements but the county was not widely settled till recent times. Good cultivation was almost confined to the Thames valley on the northern boundary, and movement across the county was limited to the Thames and the chalk uplands.

Building material, in spite of geological variety, was sparse and poor and the exploitation even of its major resource, the great southern forest, was hampered by the wet and sticky clay to north and south of the Downs and the absence till a very late

12

date of road or navigable water routes northwards to London.

Despite the wide interest of individual items in Surrey, it is therefore not surprising that neither its history nor its architecture are of national importance. Histories of England and its architecture can be, and usually are, written without any mention of the county.

Until the 19th century there were no important towns in Surrey, outside Southwark, and "memorable" events in Surrey's history, from King John's signing of Magna Carta near Egham in 1215 to the Chartists' meeting at Camberwell in 1848, were associated with events happening on the other side of the county. It has reflected rather than made the history of England. History however left its marks. The radial pattern of Roman roads from London to the ports remains: one forms the ancient boundary with Kent. The Norman kings took advantage of the wildness and made it a hunting paradise. Tudor kings dotted it with palaces and Jacobeans with racecourses. Hunting has been reduced by building and railway electrification and the palaces have been used as quarries for

Basingstoke Canal at **West Byfleet**

meaner buildings, but much of the great parks remain, while racing and other sports flourish. Modern industries spread radially from the medieval centre at Southwark as communications improved, while older industries vanished. The first native glass industry flourished in south-west Surrey in the 13th and 14th centuries and the Wealden iron industry in southern Surrey from the 14th to the 16th, before local timber was exhausted and the greater economies afforded by Forest of Dean and northern coalfields took both industries away. Woollen cloth made a number of monastic foundations in Surrey rich for a time, though manufacture is now confined to Godalming, while the making of gunpowder which was introduced by Elizabeth I and was for long a Surrey monopoly died only with the closure of the Chilworth works after World War I. Little trace of these early industries, except for the ponds that gave their motive power, can now be seen.

◁ **Frensham** Little Pond

15

Richmond Bridge

◁ The Thames at **Richmond** Lock

Chertsey Bridge

Surrey's early poverty is confirmed not only in the absence of many great buildings but in the short entry in Domesday Book (1086) and in the small 17th-century assessments for Ship Money. But the rise of its medieval industries, agricultural improvement, nearness to London and, above all, royal patronage contributed to a rising living standard which is reflected in its later medieval buildings. The buildings of the early monastic settlements, the great Abbey at Chertsey founded in 666, Waverley Abbey, the first Cistercian foundation in the country (1128), Merton Abbey, the early parish churches and the King's Castle at Guildford were all simple in design and execution.

By the 15th century, however, as can be seen from the bishops' palaces at Farnham and Croydon and the many yeomen's houses in the Weald, Surrey does not lag far behind national standards, even if it has not the number and size of buildings of its neighbour Kent.

The Reformation was a mixed blessing here. All the important monasteries, which were the biggest buildings in Surrey, were closed and their employment and education dissipated, but new "grammar schools" were founded on ex-monastic revenues, while monastic buildings were quarried for royal rebuilding at Hampton Court, Richmond and Oatlands (Weybridge), for the new palace at Nonsuch (Ewell), and for large private houses such as Loseley and Reigate. Increased interest of the Court brought harsher law, forcible enclosure and dispossession, but also new settlement, fresh in-

Some of Lutyen's work for
Jekyll at Munstead, near **Busbridge**

Tigbourne Court near **Witley**, by Lutyens 1899

vestment and some prosperity. So in spite of local discontent the county was peaceful enough by the end of the 16th century for large houses, such as Sutton Place, to be built in foreign fashions and with no further thought for defence.

Relative poverty, light soil, lack of competition from farming, and sparseness of population continued, but gave one advantage which was reaped in later centuries, for it enabled the execution of pioneer experiments in landscape design. This in turn led to the development of garden suburbs, where Surrey again led the world.

The first introduction of the Italianate

style of gardening was made by the Evelyns at Albury and Wootton in the mid 17th century; the less formal Dutch style was introduced at Moor Park, Farnham, by Sir William Temple, while the world-famous work of Hamilton and William Kent in translating the paintings of Claude into three-dimensional English landscape was done at Painshill, Esher, and Claremont. Most of the great English landscape gardeners had a hand in the fashioning of Kew Gardens, the most important in the country, where Sir William Chambers and Lancelot Brown rivalled each other in new works. Brown went on to make the largest mark of any man in the county by his work for rich patrons at Clandon, Gatton, Addington, Claremont and elsewhere and through widespread imitations by others, like the Malthus family at Westcott.

There were many bitter feuds in this field but the thread of improvement continued to the present century when the Royal Horticultural Society founded its gardens at Wisley and Wilfred Fox founded both an arboretum and the Road Beautifying Association from his home at Winkworth.

But the most memorable work of the last 100 years was done by the amateur painter and local historian, Gertrude Jekyll, who settled at Munstead in 1878, for she became the early patron of Edwin Lutyens of Thursley, the best known Surrey architect, and with him developed in practice her theories of colour perspective and the true relationship of

◁ **New Oxted**
Wonersh

p22 **Kingston-upon-Thames, Epsom** ▷
p23 **Farnham, Reigate**

house to naturalised garden. Their work was imitated by the new suburban gardeners spreading over the county by the end of the 19th century, and then throughout the country and the United States.

Surrey's prosperity began, however, with the encroachment of the metropolis on its northern territory, the growth of communications across it and the rise of middle class "commuting". In the mid-18th century Arthur Young had condemned its communications as the worst in the country, but they were rapidly improved.

The earliest move was the canalisation of the river Wey from Guildford to the Thames in 1651. The first turnpike road was made from Crawley to Reigate in 1696, though this had posts down the middle to prevent use by carriages, and in the first half of the 18th century there was a rapid spread of new roads. In the second half a spread of canals followed, the Godalming Navigation in 1760, the Basingstoke Canal in 1796 and the Wey and Arun Canal in 1813. But the canals came too late to be valuable and the last was already overtaken by the first public railway in the world, which was in Surrey from Wandsworth to Croydon in 1803 and on through the Downs to Merstham in 1805. The latter was horse-drawn but in steam railways Surrey also pioneered. The London to Woking line was opened in 1838 and was the first in the South East, and this was followed by the Croydon line via Forest Hill (which used a new canal

Caterham

bed) in 1841, extensions to Brighton in 1841, Guildford in 1845 and Portsmouth in 1849, so that by the middle of the 19th century there was a wide network of railways in the county.

The existence of London as a source of employment and the attractions of Surrey as a place of residence, joined by the new railway system, led to the biggest explosion of building in its history. Use of the county as a dormitory by rich men from London was not new; it was popular from Epsom in the early 18th century, and Cobbett roundly condemned the spread of "stockjobbers" and "City farmers" but

railways made the county accessible to a wider class of country lover; whole new towns round previously isolated stations like Horley, Surbiton and Woking were created to meet their needs.

The population of the old county, which had reached 270,000 in 1801, reached 680,000 in 1851 and well over a million by 1871. Further massive increases followed the early electrification of the suburban lines from 1910 onwards, and peak expansion of both was reached at the outbreak of World War II.

The advent of the motor-car also made its mark but not as dramatically as the

Tatsfield

railways had done. The first motor-racing track in the country was at Brooklands near Weybridge and the Kingston By-pass was one of the first 20th-century motor roads. The proportion of cars to houses rose higher than that of any other county in the country but at the same time the resistance of residents to new roads and improvements kept it backward in the highway field. The car assisted the sub-urbanisation of areas between railway lines but the "frustration factor" due to lack of road improvement kept down its usage. The square miles of "semis" seen from the Kingston By-pass were built

there not because the motor-car had made them accessible but because the areas were within walking distance of electric trains.

The view of apparently endless "semis" in fact produced a public revulsion against the spread of London and a general acceptance of the view that its further growth ought to be stopped by some "green belt". The depopulation of London in World War II, followed by the introduction of planning controls to prevent further sprawl, sharply reduced population growth in Surrey. Population of that part of the old County now within London has declined since 1939 and for

25

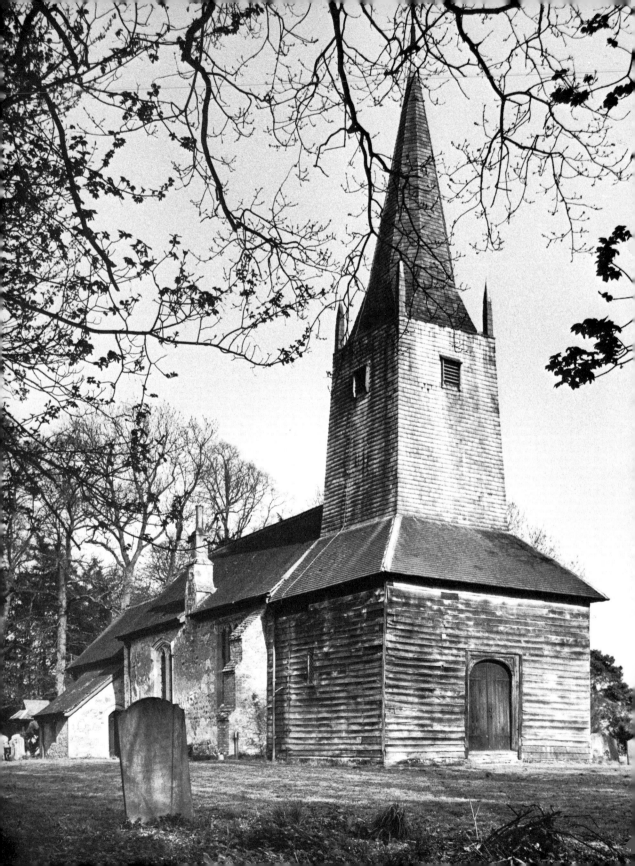

Newdigate

Crowhurst

Burstow ▷

Thames Ditton

◁ **Haxted** Mill

◁ "The White House"
Cheam

the remainder has risen much more slowly. The official designation of the Metropolitan Green Belt, and then of the "area of outstanding natural beauty" (mostly the Surrey Hills) as one to be conserved, has prevented the extermination of large areas of countryside and in spite of planned expansion of Camberley and less planned of Woking and Guildford (the latter for the new university), the pattern of development is not now so different from what it was in 1939.

"Stockjobbers and City Farmers" are still there, though many have spread to Sussex and Hampshire, but it is with their help, and with the moral support of residents of the densely populated areas, that the main and most attractive country

Witley

◁ Capel

Haslemere and **Reigate**

areas have been kept so that the county has made its greatest contribution to the metropolis by providing its closest and most enjoyable "national park". Meanwhile trees planted in early 20th-century suburbs are maturing and together with older woodlands and scattered trees everywhere make the county, in autumn golds or light greens of spring, the prettiest county in England.

"New Surrey"

Under the London Government Act 1964 the Administrative County of Middlesex disappeared. The greater part went into the new Greater London but the south-west corner was added to the administrative County of Surrey.

William Cobbett, a man of Surrey and strong prejudices, declared roundly that "all Middlesex is ugly" and particularly mentions (in his first Rural Ride) the area that now falls into Surrey. It is not the most topographically varied part of Middlesex and has none of the architectural grandeurs of Hampton Court, Osterley and Syon, which are all in Greater London, and much is frankly plain or downright ugly, but there are attractive stretches still, particularly along the Thames, while its old churches are more interesting than most in Surrey.

The area is almost level and consists (or consisted) of fine loam over layers of gravel which produced rich, well watered, well drained, land and one of the finest market garden areas in the country. Much of this has disappeared for ever to make

Shalford School (by Woodyer)
Betchworth
Abinger

Ockley

way for other development. The northern edge has gone into London's Heathrow Airport, much of the centre into giant reservoirs for London's water and much of the rest under 20th-century housing. The narrow ragged sectors of "Green Belt" between them are nearly all being worked for the remaining gravel deposits while those gravelly areas already worked out have too-often been "restored" with London's refuse to indifferent down-graded agriculture.

Several historically interesting villages are however still worth exploring by visitors, and gravel workings are now being moulded to produce a new land-scape of planted lagoons where sailing, other water sports and even nature study may flourish.

Porches:
p34 Lutyens at Pasture Wood (**Abinger**) ▷
p35 Mediaeval at **Ockley**

Gazetteer

The number after the place name refers to the square on the map following p. 192 where the place is to be found.

* Indicates a place formerly in Surrey, now in London.

** Indicates a place formerly in Middlesex, now in Surrey.

Abinger [8] the longest parish in Surrey, stretching 9½ miles from flinty woodlands on the North Downs, south across the clay Holmesdale over wild Greensand Hills to the heavy oak woodlands of the Weald.

There are two villages, Abinger Common, scattered round a thin triangular green with the church and Manor House on its west, and the better-known Abinger Hammer with its ponds and striking

clock on the Guildford–Dorking road. St James's Church, 12th and 13th century in origin, was largely rebuilt by F. Etchells in 1950. Behind the church is a Norman motte and in the field to its west are remains of a 7,000-year-old mesolithic pit dwelling. At Abinger Hammer, where Victorian tilehung houses were added to the small group of earlier buildings, are the Clock House by Milne and Hall (1891) and watercress beds, once hammer ponds of a medieval forge.

The 17th-century Crossways

Farm, with double porch and thick brick cornices on the Dorking Road, was the setting of Meredith's *Diana of the Crossways*. Abinger was a haunt of Edwardian and inter-war intellectuals such as the Webbs and E. M. Forster. They left little of architectural interest but much of their planting such as Miss Jekyll's at the Sidney Webb house (*Pasture Wood* by W. Flockhart), is worth seeing in its florid maturity. Goddards, a pretty house by E. Lutyens (1898), was designed as a ladies' home of rest.

◁ **Crossways Farm, Abinger** and (*below*) Galleting in one of the farm buildings

37

Sutton Abinger [8] A hamlet on the Holmbury road in the winding wooded valley of a Tillingbourne tributary with two 17th-century farmhouses, Fulvens Farm and Sutton Place.

Addington* [6] Plain brick cottages in a dry valley SE of Croydon islanded between hard cornfields to the S and beech woods to the N. It was favoured by 19th-century Archbishops of Canterbury, who acquired Addington Palace, a three-storey Portland stone block by Robert Mylne (1773–9), with grounds by L. Brown. They lived there from 1808 to 1896.

The church is of the 12th and 13th centuries but has been enlarged and over-restored. Inside are monuments to the Trecothicks, for whom Addington Palace was built. In the churchyard is an elaborate cross of 1911 to five Archbishops (Manners Sutton, Howley, Sumner, Longley and Tait) buried here.

New Addington* [6] The high downland S of Addington has been buried under boring modern housing.

Addiscombe* [6] The eastward, late Victorian, extension of Croydon. See the interior of St Mary Magdalene in Canning Road (E. B. Lamb 1868) for its heavy involved timber roof.

Addlestone [5] Uninteresting 19th and 20th century suburban housing squeezed between Weybridge, Chertsey and Woodham, with industry strung along the Wey. The parish church of St Paul is by James Savage (1836) of stock brick and mean. Fanny Kemble's mother Maria is buried in its churchyard. At Woburn Park was Woburn Farm once famous as a *ferme ornée* with gardens by William Kent. Woburn Hill nearby is a handsome double-bowed brick house of the early 19th century with views over Chertsey. In the town centre is the generous Civic Centre by Jellicoe, Ballantyne and Coleridge (1966), with well landscaped gardens and a gay primary school by the County Architect, R. Ash (1967).

Albury [8] A deliberately picturesque village, once known as

Albury Old Church   Some of the chimneys, **Albury** House ▷

(*above*) View SW from Newlands Corner (**Albury**)

Weston Street, which migrated down the Tillingbourne valley from the great house of Albury Park, encouraged in the 19th century by the owners of the latter. It is difficult to differentiate between the original and the early 19th-century infilling.

The old church of St Peter and St Paul stands in the Park near the house, largely disused since 1848. It is of Saxon foundation with Norman plan of nave, tower and chancel. A south transept was added in 1290, and decorated in 1839 by Pugin in red, blue and gold. The shingled dome to the tower is 15th century. The chancel is now ruined and much of the interior decayed. William Oughtred, who invented the multiplication sign ($\times$), was rector from 1610 to 1660.

Henry Drummond (1786–1860) the banker, who bought Albury in 1819, was one of the apostles of the Catholic Apostolic movement and its early meetings were held here. He built a new church for it W of the park in 1840, designed by W. M. Brookes in an incorrect Perpendicular of sandstone with W tower and chapter house. It was closed in 1950 but is well-kept. Drummond provided another church for the Weston Street settlement, also dedicated to St Peter and St Paul, in 1842 and by Brookes but in brick Romanesque. Apse and transepts were added by A. W. Blomfield in 1868. Martin Tupper (1810–89) who wrote the popular *Proverbial Philosophy* and also romantic novels about the area is buried in its churchyard.

The sixty-roomed house in Albury Park is of historical but not great architectural value, part by the brothers George and John Evelyn of Wotton who laid out most of the grounds, part by Soane, part by H. Hakewill and the whole remodelled by N. Pugin in 1846–52 who gave the house a new Tudor dress with battlements and gables and 63 varied chimneys. The result is gloomy. Cobbett, who rode through in 1822, thought the gardens "the prettiest that I ever saw in England". He saw the Park at its best for much of the planting is now over-mature—or gone.

Between the Downs and the main road (A25) is the Silent Pool, a deep clear pond overhung by trees, made famous by Martin Tupper's romance *Stephen Langton*. Newlands Corner on the crest of the Downs to the NW has one of the finest views in England, with the South Downs as back-

◁ View SE from Newlands Corner

Wey at Byfleet but the use was reduced by the railway which reached Basingstoke in 1839 and Aldershot in 1849. Great sections are dry or weed-choked as the embankment which brought water from Hampshire was closed in 1969, but there are still occasional small lakes of surprising beauty along its path, like that at Mytchett skirted by pines and oaks hiding the crowding modern subtopia and army buildings. The poet Edward Young (1683–1765) wrote *Nights Thoughts* at the Rectory.

Ashford** [2] This Ashford gave its name to the river Ash that flows round the town, instead of vice versa. It is a small parish now largely the eastern part of Staines. Till 1919 agricultural, it is now nearly all repetitive housing, the river just separating it from the similar suburban fringes of Staines proper. The parish church of St Matthew was a former chapel of Staines which was entirely rebuilt by W. Butterfield in 1858, on a site just W of the old church. The interior is severe. One brass and three medieval bells survive from the old church. St Michael's in Fordbridge Road is an incomplete church of 1928 by G. G. Scott. The Welsh Charity School, towards Staines, is the largest building in the town, stone-fronted in a Gothic style of 1857 by Henry Clutton. There are no good modern buildings and little else to interest a visitor.

Ashtead [5] Squeezed between Epsom and Leatherhead and tightly bound by its green belt, it spread in the 20th century from

ground and close set, like wings of a toy theatre, the greensand hills of St Martha's, Hascombe, Hindhead and Blackdown. On Farley Heath to the S is the overgrown site of a rare, 1st-century, Romano-Celtic temple, dug over by Martin Tupper in 1848, and more scientifically explored in 1926 and 1939.

Alfold [8] A centre for English medieval glass (see also Chiddingfold) based on charcoal made in the surrounding Wealden woods. The centre is a group of scalloped-tilehung cottages on a tiny triangular green heading towards the church of St Nicholas with its heavy Horsham slate roof and small shingled belfry supported internally by massive timber framework. The main body of the church is of the 12th, 13th and 14th centuries. The 14th has contemporary woodwork. Inside is a roughly ornamented Norman tub font and a Jacobean pulpit with sounding board. Jean le Carré,

the glass-maker from Normandy who put the Surrey forest-glass industry back on its feet in the 16th century, is buried in the churchyard (1572). Outside, stocks and whipping post still survive. There are numerous, though slight, remains of old glass works in Sidney Wood to the SW. North of the church is Alfold House, early 16th-century black and white half-timbering.

Ash [4] On the sandy ridge N of the Hog's Back, now swallowed up in the overflow of Aldershot. The church of St Peter has medieval walls, a 15th-century heath-stone tower and shingled broach spire. It was extensively restored by H. Woodyer in 1865, who added the N aisle. Inside is a 17th-century wooden font.

At Ash Vale to the N, the Basingstoke Canal enters the county from Aldershot on a long embankment across the Blackwater valley. It was opened in 1796 to connect Basingstoke to the

Betchworth

the small village on the spring line S of the chalk, expansively southwards up the chalk slopes and more closely down the heavy London clay to the railway. The church of St Giles is S of the main Epsom road, within an ancient earthwork. Norman work was incorporated in its rebuilding in 1520 and the whole was restored and enlarged in 1862 and 1891. The E window contains 16th-century glass from a Flemish monastery illustrating the crucifixion in gold and light blue. The best monuments are to Sarah Bond (1712), a Grinling Gibbons monument of 1693 to Henry Newdigate (d 1629), and a Rysbrack monument to Diana Fielding (1733). The church is on the western edge of Ashtead Park. The three-storey stock brick house now the City of London Freemen's School was designed by Bonomi in 1790 and carried out by Samuel Wyatt. Its Saloon is a circular room with alternate niches and pairs of Doric columns. To the E are the late 17th-century Park Farm House and Ashtead House. The Roman road from London to Chichester passed just S of Ashtead Park, and N from this ran another road to a Roman villa on Ashtead Common with a larger, perhaps communal, bathhouse nearby. Some of its decorated tiles have been incorporated in the church.

Bagshot [4] "Not good for little but good for nothing" was Daniel Defoe's view of the once wild, bare, heaths of Bagshot, notorious for highwaymen plaguing the Winchester and Portsmouth roads. Scots pines were introduced about 1800 and spread rapidly over the bare

heath. The better parts were enclosed for large houses and nursery gardens and the whole is now tame enough. Little of Bagshot is of any architectural note. The Church of St Anne is an ugly work of A. Cheer of 1884 decorated internally with memorials to the royal family provided by the Duke of Connaught. He lived at Bagshot Park, B. Ferrey's last work (1877) in brick and stone Tudor, now a training centre for the Army Chaplains' Service.

Hall Grove, a large house to the NE, now a boys' school, is part 18th century and earlier, having associations with Chertsey Abbey and Alexander Pope. It retains an ice-house with 30-foot diameter brick dome.

Banstead [6] Many miles of suburbia covering chalk downland, but enfolding enclaves of scrubby common and Park Downs to the SE, a small area of still attractive downland descending to the Chipstead Valley.

Racing began on Banstead Downs many years before Epsom. The centre is now neo-Tudor and neo-Georgian but the church of All Saints is of some distinction, largely late 12th century with unchamfered wide-span arcades over-restored by G. E. Street in 1868. In Banstead Wood to the S is a Norman Shaw house of many gables and star-shaped chimneys, built in 1884–90, now part of a children's hospital.

Barnes * [2] On a great bend of the Thames, built into London but still a mixed Georgian, Victorian and Edwardian village. The best parts are Church Road, the Green and the river frontage. St Mary's Church has a brick tower of the late 16th century and medieval fragments, eg the 13th-century E wall of the S aisle, but most was restored and enlarged in Victorian and later times. Outside the S wall is the grave of Edward Rose (1653), still planted

St Martins, Blackheath

with a rose-bush in accordance with his bequest. Nearby houses include the early-18th-century The Homestead (E of the church), Strawberry House to the W, and the Grange (now the Convent of the Sacred Heart— 18th century and early Victorian Gothic) and Milbourne House (18th century front but Jacobean interior), all near the Green. Facing the river are two groups of 18th-century terrace houses with iron verandahs but the riverside suffers from its road traffic and the divisive railway bridge over the Thames. To the NE are pleasant early Victorian villas, mainly handsome semi-detached with arched windows and on the river front near Hammersmith is the new St Paul's School by Bernard Feilden (1966–68) in system-built buff concrete panels and bronze

windows. The statue of the founder Dean Colet (1460–1519) was moved here from its Victorian site at Hammersmith.

Beddington* [6] A small manufacturing town on the Wandle, of great importance during the Napoleonic Wars. It is now submerged in Victorian and later suburbs of London and Croydon. The church and the Hall in Beddington Park are an oasis of peace in southern London, soon to be disturbed by the London–Crawley motorway. St Mary's, a handsome flint-faced building, in Perpendicular style, mainly of 1387 thanks to the Carews of Beddington Hall, with S (or Carew) Chapel added in the early 15th century and a second N aisle in 1852. It was restored and decorated by J. Clarke in 1869. Fittings include a 13th-

century Purbeck marble font, a pulpit of 1611, a former reredos by Clayton and Bell (1869) in the N aisle, a painted organ gallery and screen by William Morris and Co. (1869), 14th-century stalls with misericords and brasses and monuments to the Carews from 1432 onwards. Sir Walter Raleigh married a niece of the Carews and may be buried here and not at Westminster. Beddington Hall or Place was the home of the Carews from 1349 to 1762. The great hall, 16th century with hammerbeam roof where Queen Elizabeth I was entertained, has been enclosed in the red-brick Victorian school which now occupies the site. In the garden the first oranges in England were grown. There is a large 17th-century dovecote on the Park side of the Hall.

Betchworth [5] A long street set on a low sandstone ridge between Dorking and Reigate, overlooked by high Downs to the N, cradled by the river Mole to the S. St Michael's church is at the S end in a cul-de-sac of mellow brown and red cottages backed by the grounds of Betchworth House. It is largely 13th century with 11th-century fragments, but was drastically altered by E. C. Hakewill who, in 1851, removed the central Norman tower to the S aisle. The interior is dull, except for the mid-Victorian pulpit in varied marbles and mosaic panels, and the font by Eric Kennington (1952). Betchworth House is of many centuries but looks early 19th century due to alterations by T. Cundy in 1808 though the E front is more domestic Georgian. The grounds were altered by Repton and the "red book" illustrating his proposals is still kept in the house. The 16th–18th century Old House, the late

Here reſts what was
Sr ROBERT CLAYTON Kt. In the year
and at his death Alderman and Father of
and near XXX years one of its Repreſenta
the Justest Methods & Skill in Buſine
Fortune, which He applid to the Nobles
an once ventured it all for His Country
mily at Marden, where he hath left a R
e politeness of his Genius, and how
mprovd by Art. His Relations his Frien
Thomas in Southwark of which he was Preſi
the Workhouse of London, were large ſharet
in the Communion of the Church of Englan
with all Good men however divided, ar
The Welfare of his Country was the onl
actions and in all the various Efforts
time for preſerving its Constitution,
cted therein with a Constancy of
of danger could ev

s but Just the Memory of ſo Good
uld be tranſmited to after age
ublick tranſactions of his li
a pattern to imitate but h
born at Bulwick in North
ember Ano. Dom: MDCXXI
XVI day of July M
Gulielmus Clayton
Dr I

To the p
MARTHA CL
rot. of Lon
CLAYTON
Lord Mayor of

17th century "Dolphin" and the Old Mill Cottage of 16th century are also worth seeing.

Wonham Manor, about 1 mile E, is in Georgian brick Gothic by Lewis Wyatt. Betchworth Clump, 700 feet high on the crest of the North Downs, is a notable landmark above the chalk quarries in the scarp face.

For Betchworth Castle *see* Brockham.

Bisley [4] A tiny parish between sandy heath and heavy clays best known for rifle ranges (mainly in Chobham) which came here from Wimbledon Common in 1890, and an army camp (in Pirbright). St John the Baptist church standing alone in fields is of 13th century but was over-restored and enlarged in 1872. There is a 15th-century oak W porch and a Jacobean pulpit. An untidy modern village straggles along the Guildford–Bagshot road a mile to the W. The range area further W is a burnt sandy heath, the Mecca of riflemen with a special village of huge timber pavilions with verandahs like a hill station in India.

Blackheath [8] "A pretty village with hardly any peasants and the church exactly suited to such a place" (Basil Clarke), a Victorian village on the sand hills SW of Albury, adjoining wide heathlands and remote as Surrey places go. The church of St Martin is by C. H. Townsend, 1895, with frescoes by Mrs Lea Merritt. To the N in pine woods is the Franciscan monastery of Greyfriars, incorporating stone church and dormitories under one roof by F. A. Walters (1895). To the S is The Hallams (Norman Shaw, 1895).

Bletchingley [6] Once a market town, and a borough until the Reform Act 1832, now largely one wide, curving village street—the best in Surrey—on the sandy ridge E of Redhill. The church of St Mary is largely 15th century but the W tower is Norman, heightened in the 17th century, and the whole has been much altered. In the S chapel is the monument by Richard Crutcher to Sir Robert Clayton (d 1707) and his wife, with over-life-size figures in an aedicule filling the E wall, one of the best early 18th monuments in the country. A reredos by G. E. Street (1870) has a figure of Bishop Wilberforce among apostles. The High Street is punctuated by modest gabled and tilehung buildings, a good inn, the 16th-century Whyte Harte, refronted at the end of the 18th, and some nasty infill of 1969 on the S, and some better on the N, where it is visually more important. Castle Hill, with its long views S over a wide area of Weald, has fragments of the Clares' stronghold demolished in 1264.

Blindley Heath [9] A ribbon of houses on the Roman Road (now A22) S of Godstone. St John's Church is by J. Whichcord and Walker (1842) with an apsidal chancel added in 1886. Red Barn in Tandridge Lane is a 15th-century hall house altered in 1689.

Great Bookham [5] One of the string of spring-like villages N of the chalk between Guildford and Leatherhead. Since World War II gross expansion of it and Fetcham has turned it into a rather unattractive suburb of Leatherhead. Luckily heavy clay commons to the N are in the hands of the National Trust as is much of the chalk cornfields to the S.

The church of St Nicholas makes some amends. It has a weatherboarded W tower and shingled spire. The lower flint-faced stage of the tower is late 12th century, as is the N arcade with its octagonal piers. The chancel was built by the abbot of Chertsey in 1341 and the aisles were widened in the 15th century. The church was restored by R. C. Carpenter in 1845 and W. Butterfield in 1885. There are brasses of 15th, 16th and 17th centuries and 13th-century monuments. In the chancel is a Gothic tablet to Elizabeth Andrewes (1816), framed by a weeping willow in low relief as high as the chancel, with an iron railing round its foot.

The old Rectory to the W was often visited by Jane Austen. Fanny Burney (1752–1840) set up house in Fairfield House (now The Hermitage), an 18th-century cottage in Lower Road and here wrote *Camilla*, whose financial success enabled her to build her own house at Westhumble.

S of Bookham, on park-downland is Polesden Lacey, a Regency house built by Thomas Cubitt in 1824 and extended and refitted for Mrs Ronald Greville, the Edwardian hostess, by Méwès and Davis in 1906, on the site of a Carolean house owned by R. B. Sheridan from 1797 until his death in 1816. The long terrace with its view south to Ranmore Common woods was constructed by Sheridan. The house is now a monument to a great collector and her rich Edwardian way of life. The hall incorporates the reredos from the Wren city church of St Matthew Friday Street (demolished 1881), as a great overmantel to the fireplace containing 17th-century woodwork from Sheridan's house. The drawing-room in Louis-Quatorze style and the library with Ionic pilasters are the best of the

Polesden Lacey (see **Great Bookham**)
(*above*) The East Front. (*Below and opposite*) The
park and gardens

Edwardian rooms. The estate, with the house and its paintings (eg the Raeburn portraits), tapestries, furniture and china was given to the National Trust in 1942.

At the N end of the parish and facing Stoke D'Abernon across the Mole is Slyfield House. Only the SE and NW angles of a large quadrangle, now two separate houses, remain, part still retaining a 16th-century frame but all cloaked in elaborate brickwork of 1615–40. The S front of the SE house has a large shaped Dutch gable on the W and seven slightly later bays to the E, divided by giant pilasters decorated with badges. Inside decorative plasterwork ceilings with writhing swags, birds and strapwork of 1625, a staircase of 1640 with rusticated newel posts, and strapwork panels.

Little Bookham [5].

Bungalows from Great Bookham have overflowed its eastern boundary. The rest is rural.

The church lies off the road on footpath to Effingham, a single 12th-century space capped by a small belfry. There are blocked Norman arches on the S side indicating a once larger church. It was restored in 1864 and little of interest remains except the tub font bound with iron straps and a minor monument of 1812.

Bourne [7]

A hamlet in the Bourne valley now swallowed in southern suburbs of Farnham. "George Bourne", born Sturt (1863–1927), author of The Wheelwright's Shop (1923), took his pseudonym from this, his birthplace. At St Thomas's Church, an unfinished, indifferent, design by H. Sidebotham, 1911, is the grave of H. D. Waghorn, the Schneider Trophy pilot who reached 329 mph.

Brewer Street Farmhouse

Box Hill [5]

The best-known beauty spot in Surrey, a high-point on the Downs N of Dorking with view S over the Weald to the sandhills and South Downs and more intimate views over the Mickleham valley and Ranmore to the W, named from the native box trees which still clothe the western cliff to the river Mole. It was the scene of the picnic in Jane Austen's *Emma*. At Flint Cottage, at the western foot of the hill, George Meredith lived from 1867 to his death in 1909.

Over 900 acres are held by the National Trust but to the E many acres of hill-top caravan sites give warning of what might have happened here. On the NW side, Juniper Hall, a field-study centre (National Trust 1945) was the home of Talleyrand, Mme de Staël and other French emigrés, at the time of the Revolution and here Fanny Burney met General D'Arblay. Though set in mature cedars, the house is not attractive, but it contains a drawing-room in Adam style with repeated Wedgwood plaques.

Bramley [7]

A large village S of Guildford, harshly extended by Victorians after the coming of the railway in 1865 and made worse in this century, still contains a core of 18th and early 19th century solid brick houses with walls and trees. Holy Trinity Church is a dull building with Norman fragments and a 13th-century chancel. The rest is of 1850 and 1875. A monument to Henry Ludlow (1730) in the S aisle has a large urn and flambeau set in a Palladian frame.

The country around with little fields rising steeply to round wooded hills is all attractive but especially up the valley towards Thorncombe Street. The road there leads past the formidable tilehung timber and brick Snowdenham Hall by Ralph Nevil (1868 and 1887), the 16th-century half-timbered Nurscombe Farm and the demure late-Georgian stuccoed Thorncombe Park, while to the W is Unstead Park, on a wooded hill overlooking Godalming, a well-detailed brown-brick house of 1780, occupied by Lord John

Russell in the mid 19th century. Thorncombe Street is a hamlet of half-timbered cottages south of Thorncombe Park. The deepest wind-cut road in Surrey, exposing some 30 feet of greensand, ascends from here towards Munstead.

Brewer Street [6] A hamlet one mile N of Bletchingley in the Holmesdale between sand hills and chalk downs. Here are the pretty, close-timbered, 15th-century Brewer Street Farmhouse, with a hipped Horsham slate roof and a central hall, now divided, and 18th-century Place Farm, with Tudor brick arch marking the site of the great gatehouse of Bletchingley Place, the home of Anne of Cleves.

Brockham [5] An overgrown village, straggling in all directions from its green, famous for the view of Box Hill rising to the N framed between pretty cottages and trees. Christ Church, by B. Ferrey (1846) in a cruciform neo-13th century style, fills the picture to the S. There are a number of good minor houses and farmhouses in and around, eg the late 18th-century Brockham Court to the E, and the 17th-century Feltons Farm to the SW. Betchworth Castle, on the Dorking side of the Mole W of Brockham has fragmentary walls of the castle built by Sir Thomas Browne in 1449, and later converted to a manor house. The stables to the N in neat flint and brick are by Soane (1799).

Brook [7] A hamlet of sandstone and half-timbered cottages on the Godalming–Haslemere Road. The neo-Tudor Brook Lodge with a copper-roofed dovecote, N of the hamlet, is a relic of a large house in Witley Park, built about the turn of the century, for Whitaker Wright, a Victorian financier. A colonnaded stone boat-house by Lutyens survives in its park.

Brookwood [4] A product of the railway age with a huge cemetery. An area of barren heathland along the Southampton railway was laid out by Sir William Tite and Sydney Smirke

Witley Park, **Brook**: The boathouse by Lutyens

for the London Necropolis Co., with private railway stations, and opened in 1852. It was then the largest graveyard in the world. Early Victorian planting, now mature, makes the estate one of the most picturesque in Surrey. Visually best is the military area to the NE, and in particular the U.S. section, by E. Swartout (1929) with a long evergreen-bordered lawn leading to a classical mausoleum.

The village, largely in hot Woking brick, lies on the N between the railway and the Basingstoke canal.

Buckland [5] A tidy village round a small tidy green spoilt by traffic on the bisecting A25 between Dorking and Reigate. The church on the S side has a medieval shingled belfry and walls of dark, almost purple, sandstone. All but the belfry are Woodyer's solid rebuilding of 1860, pretty inside and out. There are 14th-century stained-glass figures of Saints Peter and Paul in dark reds and blues in the nave. Second-best is the 17th-century Streets Farm on the W side with black-boarded barn capped by turret and running-fox weathervane.

Burpham [5] A NE suburb of Guildford. St Luke's is an aisleless chapel by H. Woodyer of 1859.

Burstow [9] Scattered development in rather dull Wealden clay. The church of St Bartholomew stands almost alone in a quiet (when Gatwick Airport allows) lane set closely with trees. Its medieval timber tower and belfry is built up on four corner-posts with diagonal bracing wrapped in a weatherboarded skirt. The upper stage is battered and rises to a slender broach spire with four corner spirelets, all shingled. The rest of the church is in mainly Norman golden sandstone with

Perpendicular details. Inside is an octagonal 15th-century font and a formidable late 16th-century chest bound with vertical iron strips. John Flamsteed (1646–1719), the first Astronomer Royal, who held the living, is buried in the chancel. Old Court, S of the church is a 16th-century moated house rebuilt in 1786. The parish is large and includes overspill of the Sussex village of Copthorne (with nothing worth noting on the Surrey side) to the S and the unattractive settlement of Smallfield to the N. Smallfield Place to its E is a stone-built manor house (unusual in Surrey) of the late 16th century, rebuilt in 1665 (and now divided into two) with a fine porch and oriel windows. Burstow Lodge, N. of Smallfield, still retains the structure of its 14th-century hall. Further N and still in this parish is Outwood (qv).

Busbridge [7] An overspill of large Victorian and Edwardian houses on to wooded sandhills S and E of Godalming. The parish swings from Tuesley, with its ugly early 20th-century hospital, SE to the fringe of Hascombe and then N to Munstead with its Lutyens houses and Jekyll gardens.

St John the Baptist church by G. G. Scott, 1868, is local (Burgate) sandstone with a shingled centre tower. Its fittings include stained glass in E and W windows by Burne-Jones (1899) and a combined ironwork chancel-screen and rood designed by E. Lutyens (1899). Outside, the war memorial is also by Lutyens, as is the memorial to Gertrude Jekyll, and her brother (Sir Herbert Jekyll) and sister-in-law. Gertrude Jekyll (1843–1932), the historian of West Surrey, landscape artist and early patron of Lutyens, led the revolt against the heavy formal gardens of her times. She lived for over 30 years at Mun-

stead Wood, a U-shaped house, built for her by Lutyens in 1896 in a free Tudor style. Opposite this is his earlier Munstead Place (1891) and to the NE is Orchards, his best house, of 1899. The last is built in stone cut like bricks (a feature of much 18th-century West Surrey building) round a quadrangle with an extension producing an L-shaped entrance. Gertrude Jekyll collaborated with Lutyens in the design of the gardens of all three.

Busbridge Hall, SW of the church, was a Palladian house of 1775, rebuilt in a gabled-style fashionable in 1906. The stables of the old house were made into a separate house but the grounds retain its ornamental lakes, 18th-century planting and ornaments, bridges, grotto and temple.

Byfleet [5] A jumble of streets in flat land between the old river Wey and the newer "Navigation", made much uglier since World War II. St Mary has late 13th-century nave, chancel and belfry, a S aisle added in 1841 and S transept (by H. Woodyer) in 1864. There is a fading painting of a seated king, possibly Edward II, who held the manor here, on N wall. Joseph Spence, friend of Pope, and George Smith, founder of the *Dictionary of National Biography*, are buried in the churchyard. To the SE, hidden among trees by the Wey, is the Manor House, in mellow 17th-century brick, a delightful surprise framed in tall urn-capped gate-piers. Parts of the house of Anne, Queen of James I, the Jacobean pilasters and a huge W chimney, are incorporated in the present five-bay, two-storey, house.

West Byfleet [5] A pre-war stockbrokers' retreat with wide straight roads and widely spaced houses nicely planted up. St John the Baptist with a shingled steeple is by W. D. Caröe (1912). N of the railway is a section of the Basingstoke Canal with a long line of black and white houseboats moored in its rather stagnant waters.

Camberley [4] Gentle pine-wooded hills descend in waves to the Hampshire–Berkshire boundary on the Blackwater, where the Basingstoke road divides the grounds of the Royal Military Academy and the Royal Staff College on the N from the town to the S. Everything, from the pine trees to the town's name, is 19th century or later. The R.M.A. came from Marlow in 1812 and its large staff houses and neo-Doric lodges by J. Wyatt are on the Surrey side along the Basingstoke road. York Town, the older part of the town, grew on a grid pattern of the R.M.A. while the more generous landscape of curving roads, large houses, big trees and rhododendrons to the SE followed the establishment of the Staff College in 1862.

The church of St Michael, by H. Woodyer 1851, with Burgate stone tower and broach spire, stands between the two colleges, on a wooded knoll above the main road, while the newer church by Caröe (1902) with belfry and sharp gables is set against a background of pines in Church Hill.

The Staff College is a large simple block in stone and stock brick and Louis XIV style, with a centre decorated with florid trophies, by James Pennethorne. Prince Albert contracted his last illness while admiring its construction. The town presents its worst face to the main road, and new development in the town centre is not improving it, but the winding suburban roads of Upper Camberley are still beautiful, in spite of redevelopment and massive infilling.

Capel [8] Tilehung and weather-boarded old cottages and modern bungalows strung out along the gentle windings of the London–Worthing road stop on the steep wooded hill at its S end. St John's church at the centre is 13th century but largely rebuilt by Woodyer in 1865 with a shingled, spired, belfry. Inside there is an early Victorian font and Cowper monuments.

Wealden timber-framed farm-houses are scattered around, notably Bonets and Osgoods to the S, Taylors to the SE and Aldhurst, Misbrooks and Temple Elfande to the E. Osgoods has wings by Lutyens, Taylors a 14th-century hall.

Carshalton* [6] The ponds, fed by chalk springs, which were gently tamed in the 18th century with graceful brick and stone bridges, and surrounded with trees and seats, make the centre of Carshalton an oasis in miles of outer London suburbs. The church of All Saints lies on a hillock on the S side where it appears largely Victorian, thanks to rebuilding by the Blomfields, though happily composed with its medieval tower and 18th-century spirelet. The nave of the medieval church, now a S aisle, faces the quiet, well-treed, graveyard at the back. Inside are a rood screen and organ case by Ninian Comper of 1933, and monuments from the 15th century on, notably the tomb of Nicholas Gaynesford (1497) with kneeling brass figures, Sir John Fellowes (1724) and John Bradyll (1753) by Rysbrack.

The grand Carshalton House was built at the W end of the ponds early in the 18th century, three storeys high, of nine by seven bays, in yellow and red brick with pilasters in rubbed red brick and a hipped roof. The interior has a pillared entrance hall and a number of other fine rooms. The

gardens were laid out by Charles Bridgeman for Fellowes of the South Sea Company, who bought the house in 1716, in the then new picturesque style with a lake and grotto and a tall water-tower, but much of these have gone under the late Victorian buildings of the present Convent. The road from Epsom to Croydon, while bringing unwelcome traffic, provides a dramatic entrance to the village centre as it swings round the high walls of the House past its entrance gates with lions' heads, past the weatherboarded Greyhound Inn and alongside the ponds and bridges. Just N of the ponds, in Festival Walk, is the old Rectory, an early 18th-century house, in red and blue brick check with a pedimented doorway. The grounds of the Grove enfold the eastern pond and a little low segmented arched stone bridge mistakenly called the "Leoni bridge".

Weatherboarded cottages from the old village still stand in North and West Streets. In Carshalton Park S of the centre are a temple and grotto from another early 18th-century garden layout, while in Oaks Park nearly two miles S was the house built for Lord Derby after which the annual fillies' race at Epsom was named. This had a magnificent supper pavilion by Robert Adam, demolished in 1960.

Caterham [6] There are still two villages, the old on the now urbanised downland and the Victorian built in the pretty wooded valley below. The railway came up the valley from Croydon in 1856 and new Caterham spread on the valley side till it joined the old. Then, between the World Wars, development spread up the downland from Coulsdon and joined the Old to London. The flint village church of St Lawrence on the hill was built at the end of

the 11th century but much altered in the 12th and 13th and extended in the 18th century. It is now disused, for much larger flint-faced church, St Mary's, was built on the opposite side of the road in 1866 by W. and C. A. Basset Smith, and enlarged in 1883 and 1916. The 126 foot high spire was added in 1883. The reredos and an iron screen to the chancel are by Comper—The 13th-century font is from the old church. In the Valley, another new church, that of St John, was built by W. Basset Smith in 1881, in sandstone with a big W tower.

The Valley has large late Victorian houses in either Norman or Tudor style set in large gardens and in spite of recent indifferent infilling the view over the Valley from the Hill is still attractive.

On the downland the Guards Barracks, begun in 1877, are better than adjoining development round Old Caterham, and the chapel by W. Butterfield of 1886, with patterns of black bricks and flint panels, is one of his best works.

To the S is Tupwood Gorse, the house built (1873) by Philip Webb for Queen Victoria's dentist, and beyond on the Downs crest is a noted viewpoint looking over Godstone and Bletchingley to the Central Weald from Ashdown Forest to Leith Hill, while below to the SW in a fold in the chalk is the hidden valley of Quarry Hanger, with a rare expanse of downland turf below steep beech wood.

Chaldon [6] There is not much of a village to this place on the high downland W of Caterham but an overspill of Caterham housing to the E and scattered small houses. The church of St Peter and St Paul stands almost alone to the NW, a small 12th- and early 13th-century flint building with a

SW stone tower and broach spire of 1843. A unique "Doom" painting of about 1200, rediscovered in 1870 beneath coats of whitewash, covers the whole W wall of the interior. Aesthetically, and theologically, grotesque it pictures figures in Hell and Purgatory with a ladder to a wavy Heaven above. Devils, angels and humans are in white and yellow on a red ochre background, while the seven deadly sins are illustrated, eg luxury by a devil interrupting an embracing couple, in odd angles. The pulpit is dated 1657. The 18th-century exterior of the adjoining Chaldon Court hides its 14th-century origins and medieval hall.

Charlwood [8] A large parish which seems, with its heavy oak and elm hedgerows, gentle undulations and glimpses of distant Downs, to be deep country. The centre is a picturesque group of tilehung, timber-framed cottages and golden sandstone church approached over local limestone paving. The tower and N and W walls of the original nave date from 1080. A wide S aisle was added in the late 13th century and a porch and S chapel in the late 15th, when the S aisle was enlarged to form the present nave. The whole was restored by Burges in 1858. On the S wall are considerable late 13th-century wall-paintings of St Margaret of Antioch (E) and St Nicholas and Three Living and Three Dead (W), which have faded steadily since they were uncovered in 1858. The screen is the best medieval woodwork in Surrey, given by Richard Sanders (d 1480) whose initials with angels holding the letters IHS and a crowned M are worked into its design. The pulpit is mixed Tudor and Jacobean. There are large houses scattered around; Charlwood House (towards Low-

field Heath) is L-shaped timber-framed and close-studded 15th century; Charlwood Park Farm House is 15th century half-timbered, and Charlwood Place, a half H-shaped building of the 16th and 19th century was built by the Sanders family and originally moated.

The whole of London's second airport, Gatwick, is contained within this parish, and it has already cut off and destroyed much of Lowfield Heath.

Hookwood [8] Mainly 20th-century ribbon development along the Reigate–Brighton Road N of Gatwick Airport, with a few old buildings, eg the 17th-century timber-framed, brick and tile-floored Hookwood House, occupied by the Sanders family (see Charlwood) from the 17th century.

Cheam * [6] A huge suburb, Siamese twin of Sutton, with a gentle slope down to the N. Larger houses are on chalk to the S, smaller on clay to the N. In the centre are mock-Tudor shops, but also some old weatherboarded cottages from the tiny pre-19th-century village and one large house, Whitehall in Malden Road, whose history can be traced back to the 15th century. Timber-framed and gabled but not weatherboarded till the 18th century, it has been carefully restored and is now a local arts centre. The nearby church of St Dunstan was totally rebuilt by G. A. Pownall in 1864, in florid Gothic. The separate, much altered, flint chancel of the medieval church is well preserved in the churchyard and called the Lumley chapel. Its interior should be seen for the plaster-decorated ceiling and tie beams done in 1592, its brasses (eg the palimpsest of Thomas Fromonde of 1542), and the family monuments erected for Baron

Lumley, Lord Chamberlain to Elizabeth I. These are a table tomb to his first wife, Jane Fitzalan (1577), an alabaster effigy of his second, Elizabeth D'Arcy (1592) and a larger framed plate to himself (d 1609). Cheam School, famous for its 18th-century head William Gilpin ("Dr Syntax") and pupils Lord Randolph Churchill and the Duke of Edinburgh, moved here from London in 1665 and stood till 1934 (when it was moved to Berkshire) just S of the road to Sutton.

On the Ewell side is Nonsuch Park, remnant of the great enclosure round the Tudor palace of Nonsuch. The present house of that name (nearly a mile E of the site of the Palace) is a turreted house by J. Wyattville of 1802–6.

Chelsham [6] A parish of high chalk fields and small woods on the Kent border. Modern Chelsham is an overflow of Warlingham around a large bus garage on the Westerham Road within the parish of Warlingham. N of the Westerham Road are scattered flint and brick cottages round a bushy green and N again is the Warlingham Park mental hospital, by Oatley and Skinner (1902) with polychrome brick tower peering over surrounding woods. The parish church of St Leonard is another mile E by itself down an avenue of beech trees near the head of a small combe, an aisleless church in medieval flint, ruthlessly restored in 1871. The font is a 13th-century square bowl of Bethersden marble and there is a mid-16th-century screen to the chancel which combines Gothic tracery and renaissance columns. Royal Arms of Elizabeth II make a rare but welcome addition to the church. Little of architectural interest is left in the area but further N the large early 18th-century Fickleshole Farm, and the

over-embellished White Bear Inn and adjoining cottages form a pleasant group.

Chertsey [2] A small town of 18th- and 19th-century houses near the Thames, once renowned for its great Benedictine Abbey, the earliest religious house in Surrey, founded in AD 666. Patronised by Mercian kings, but wiped out by Danish raiders in the 9th century, it was rebuilt in the 10th to become rich and important. The Abbey lay N of the present town centre and blocked development in that direction so that the present main streets form a T. The latest Abbey church was begun in 1110 and finished in the next century. Its plan uniquely combined English and French practice by having an ambulatory around a square east end with apsidal chapels leading off it. The Abbey was dissolved in 1538 and only a few rubble stone walls, an arch, parts of a barn to the N, and fragments of the Abbey church foundation in a garden rockery remain, because the materials were used for the building of the Tudor palaces at Oatlands and Hampton Court a few miles downstream. A large house was built in the site (with some remaining fragments of the Abbey) by Sir Nicholas Carew of Beddington in the 17th century but this too has vanished. The Abbey fishponds can be seen in the small park N of the Staines Road; the rest of the site can be seen, where not covered with modern houses, by taking the path N alongside the parish Church of St Peter.

The latter stands by the main road junction and is disappointingly uninteresting for a place of medieval importance. It retains a medieval tower of rubble stone and brick patches and a medieval chancel, but all the detail has been renewed while the main body is a

large hall with wide vaults held on square iron piers encased in wooden shafts, in poor Gothic by R. Elsam and then T. Chawner of 1806–8. The vaults were decorated with floral panels in T. G. Jackson's extensive restoration of 1907. There are a few encaustic tiles from the Abbey, for which it was once world-renowned, set in the S chapel (better examples can be seen in the Guildford Museum) and there is a monument to Emily Mawbey (1819) by Flaxman. From the church westward, Windsor Street has a number of early 18th-century houses. In the centre of the best group on the N side is Curfew House, in a Vanbrughish style of 1725, taller and slightly set back from the others. It was built as a school and the tympanum is inscribed "Founded by Sr Wm Perkins Knt. for Fifty Children clothed and taught. Go and do likewise". London Street with its jolly Italianate town hall of 1851 runs eastwards into Bridge Street and so to the river crossing a mile away. The bridge itself is a beautiful stone structure of seven arches (1775) by James Paine, who lived at Sayes Court nearby. It was partly rebuilt in 1894.

Upstream is Chertsey Lock, then the bridge for the Basingstoke motorway (1970) designed by R. Parry and C. Theobald, and then one of the best sailing reaches on the Thames in Surrey. Back in the centre, Guildford Street runs S of the church, and contains most of the modern shopping set in mutilated 18th- and 19th-century houses. No. 59 (on the W side) was the site of Porch House where Abraham Cowley, Royalist poet (1618–67), spent his last years (after moving from Barnes) "stretched at ease in Chertsey's silent bowers". To the west is Pyrcroft House, mid-18th century with brick pilasters capped with stone vases. One mile further W

58

Chilworth

is St Ann's Hill made famous in 18th-century poetry. Charles James Fox (1749–1806) lived in a house on the S side which has been replaced by an elegant house of 1936 by Raymond McGrath in then "international" style while the mature 18th-century gardens were improved by the landscape architect Christopher Tunnard.

The Thames plain around Chertsey, now pock-marked with gravel ponds, was once renowned for its market gardens and the first carrots were introduced into England here.

Chessington* [5] A long wedge of inter-war and post-war housing starting at Hook on the Kingston By-pass and ending in the green belt at Burnt Stub Zoo, whose entrance is incongruously marked by an old London tram. The zoo specialises in entertaining children but has gardens, a penguin pool and an ape-house with adult appeal. Its H.Q. is in the old house originally built in 1348, burnt down in 1645 and 1919 but still incorporating fragments of both buildings. The church of St Mary is near Chessington South Station, tiny, of medieval origin but over-restored and enlarged in the 19th century. At the W end is a tablet to Dr Samuel Crisp who owned Chessington Hall where his friend Dr Burney's daughter Fanny (*see* Gt Bookham) wrote much of her best-selling novels *Evelina* (1778) and *Cecilia* (1782).

Chiddingfold [7] A large village in deep-wooded country near the Sussex border, the centre of the medieval forest glass industry. It developed round a large irregular green with the church of St Mary, the pond and the Crown Inn at its focal point near the southern end. The big W tower of the church and its high 15th-century arcades are noteworthy but most antiquarian interest was removed in Woodyer's restoration (1869). In the W window set in an abstract pattern are fragments of local medieval glass, collected from sites of disused glass-houses. Such sites can still be traced in Vann Copse, Hazelbridge Hanger and Ramsnest Common to the S. This West Surrey industry used local sand, bracken and charcoal and was introduced by the Normans in 1226; it lasted until about 1615 when new methods and the use of coal in the Midlands and Forest of Dean caused its collapse.

Of the attractive buildings in the village the Crown Inn is the most interesting. It is a large timber-framed building known as an Inn since the 14th century and probably the oldest pub in

Surrey. The beams are aggressively exposed outside but were hidden by the traditional hung tiles of Southern Surrey until after World War II.

Pickhurst to the SW is a large tilehung, half-timbered, house in Norman Shaw style by J. M. Brydon (1883).

In the Forestry Commission's "Chiddingfold Forest" the making of walking-sticks from knotted ash saplings survives.

Chilworth [8] "This valley . . . one of the choicest retreats of man, perverted to the making of gunpowder and banknotes." So Cobbett in 1822. The valley, that of the Tillingbourne winding gently through wooded sandstone hills, remains lovely and the gunpowder and banknote factories have gone. But the village street, a 19th- and 20th-century ribbon of houses along the Dorking–Godalming road, is one of the ugliest in Surrey. The parish church is St Martha, alone but prominent on St Martha's Hill. Its Norman walls damaged by a powder-works explosion were rebuilt and enlarged by Woodyer in 1850. It is now a simple cruciform Burgate-stone building incorporating details from the old church such as the late 12th-century pointed crossing arches. The 12th-century tub-shaped font with 19th-century decoration came from Hambledon.

There are a number of prehistoric earthworks on the hill and a tradition of the burial of Christian martyrs here in the 7th century so it seems likely that the hill's name is a corruption of Martyrs.

Chilworth Manor, the most important house in the parish, lies between St Martha and the village, built in mid-17th-century brick for the gunpowder manufacturer Vincent Randyll and enlarged in 1725 and later. In terraces up the hill is the 17th-century walled garden reminiscent of the Evelyn's work at Albury.

At Shalford Hamlet is a church built as an Institute by W. H. Seth-Smith (1896).

Chipstead [6] Scattered development over chalk downland; tight suburbia to the N round the deep Chipstead Valley (in Woodmansterne parish), more leafy and villagey on the high ground to the S but almost without architectural or historic interest save for the church of St Margaret. This stands alone to the S by a triangular green on high ground near the Brighton motorway, a large flint-faced building, mainly 13th century but with work of the 12th century incorporated. The central tower is dated 1631, the S transept was rebuilt in mid-19th century and the N aisle by Norman Shaw, who added the pretty neo-Perpendicular W door in 1883. Inside are well-proportioned Early English arcades in Reigate stone, a big 14th-century font, 15th-century chancel screen, Jacobean pulpit, fragments of medieval glass in the E window, stone benches along the N and S walls of the chancel, its triangular-headed lancet windows, and monuments to J. Tattershall (1784) by R. Westmacott and to the contractor Sir Edward Banks (1835).

Chobham [4] The largest parish in Surrey with the county's largest common to the N, and untidy farmland grading into Woking suburbs to the S.

The church of St Lawrence, of many ages and externally attractive thanks to the warm and varied hues of its stonework, is spoilt internally by too much restoration. The W tower of local sandstone with crude dressings, capped with a lead spike, dominates the village centre. Inside the early 12th-century arcade has massive square and round pillars and slightly pointed arches. The N aisle, chancel and S transept are late 19th century. There is a rare wooden font of unknown date, with a late 17th-century cover, and a 13th-century chest. In the chancel under an uninscribed blue stone lies Nicholas Heath, Archbishop of York 1556–60, Lord Chancellor under Mary I, who retired to Chobham Park (now gone) on the accession of Elizabeth I and was often visited by her there. There are pleasant cottages in the village and good farms and houses in the neighbourhood such as Brook Place a mile W, 17th-century brick with decorative gables, the late 17th-century Chobham Park Farm and the 16th-century Stanners Hill Farm to the E of the village and Castle Grove House, dated 1643, in brick classical to the S. To the NW at Valley End is the little chapel of St Saviour by G. F. Bodley (1867) in brick with a shingled belfry.

Chobham Common separates the village from the lusher residential areas of Sunningdale and Virginia Water and is the most barren spot left in Surrey, a wide exposure of Bagshot sands, infertile, short of water and covered with stunted or burnt birch, heath and gorse. The popular attraction of its size and its wildness have both been badly diminished by a tank-testing ground at one end and the Basingstoke motorway across the middle.

Churt [7] A village of tilehung and sandstone, or brick, cottages with some larger Victorian houses hidden in nearby woods, nestling between the lower sandy commons of Frensham and the higher sandy commons of Hindhead. The sandy areas are pine and heath-clad but through Churt runs a band of more fertile land. The statesman David Lloyd George (1867–1945) settled here at Bron-y-De, an unattractive house by Philip Tilden of 1921, and carried out experiments with potatoes and fruit. He left Churt in 1944 having spoilt much of the country around with scattered building. The church of St John was built to designs by Ewan Christian in 1868.

East Clandon [5] The last real village left between Guildford and Leatherhead, largely the farming estate of the large house, Hatchlands, on its E. The church of St Thomas is small with 12th-century nave walls, rough Early English chancel and lean-to aisle and shingled belfry added by T. G. Jackson in 1900. Inside are an 18th-century font, late 17th-century communion rail and the neo-Jacobean tomb-chest with canopy of Lord Rendel (1913) by H. S. Goodhart-Rendel. The Rendels are descendants of Admiral Boscawen (1711–61), for whom the simple Palladian, plum-red brick, house of Hatchlands was built in 1757. Fine ceilings and other decorations in each of the principal rooms were added by Robert Adam, as one of his earliest commissions, in 1759. Alterations were made by J. Bonomi in 1790, the Wren-like porch to the E front was added by H. Ricardo in 1889 and the single-storey Wren-style music room on the N by R. Blomfield in 1903. The property was given to the National Trust in 1945.

West Clandon [5] A N–S village straggling along the Woking–Dorking road, of pretty

cottages and later houses broken up by large gardens and trees; the best are at the S end near the church of St Peter and St Paul. The church has nave walls of 13th century but was ruthlessly restored in the 19th century. The N tower and spire were added in 1879. There are medallions of 17th-century stained glass set among some of the 19th, and a 17th-century pew for the Onslow family who lived at Clandon Park.

Clandon Park lies just W. The original was a large U-shaped Jacobean house of 1642 but was entirely rebuilt for the Onslows in 1731–35 by the Italian, G. Leoni. The house is a simple rectangle but with four dissimilar elevations in red brick with stone dressings and a clumsy *porte-cochère* added in 1876. The entrance hall in strict Palladian style and symmetry, two storeys high showing superimposed Corinthian orders, has two good overmantels by Rysbrack, a Baroque plaster ceiling by Artari and painted panels by F. Barlow and is one of the best early Palladian rooms in the country. The other rooms and the modest staircase have less grandeur but were colourfully restored in 1970. The park was landscaped by L. Brown (1775) and the present stables are also by him but later alterations have cut across the design and much, now separated from the house which was bequeathed to the National Trust, is decayed or swept away. Near the house, however, are an early 18th-century flint and brick grotto with statues of the Three Graces and a complete 18th-century Maori house in bright-red and grey, brought from New Zealand.

Claygate [5] A large cul-de-sac of nondescript suburban housing round a railway station (1885)

ringed by green belt commons and farmland.

The mid-19th-century Holy Trinity enlivens it with a turret-flanked neo-Romanesque apse, as does Ruxley Towers to the E with its early 19th-century Gothic tower and frightening gargoyles.

The Semaphore House on Telegraph Hill to the N is one, with those at Guildford and Ockham, of the series built in 1822 to link Portsmouth with the Admiralty.

Cobham [5] Church Cobham on the Leatherhead road and Street Cobham on the London–Portsmouth road, in a great bend of the river Mole, have been plastered together with 20th-century infilling. The church of St Andrew, down the lane to Downside, retains its Norman W tower in stone and flint and a Norman S door, but the rest was mutilated in alterations of the 19th century. There are two interesting brasses, one of a nativity (S of chancel) and another with a figure of an early 16th-century priest and a palimpsest of a bearded knight in armour of the late 16th (on the arch between S aisle and S chapel).

Beside the church are Church Stile House in 15th-century timbering, with a double overhang rare in Surrey, and houses of the 17th and 18th centuries. Gwilt's bridge of 1782 just W was replaced after 1968 floods by a simple concrete slab. There is nothing left of note in the High Street. (The last building of interest there, a complicated rustic timber cottage crossbred from Swiss and Maori huts, was demolished in 1969.)

The best group of buildings in Cobham is in Mill Road by the Mole where are the early 19th-century mill, The Cedars, a 15th-century house with mid-

Clandon Park, **West Clandon**. The Three Graces.

18th-century brick front and elaborate gatepiers and ironwork to the road (owned by the National Trust) and the early 18th-century Ham Manor.

In Street Cobham only the White Lion, a mid-18th-century coaching house at the bend in the Portsmouth Road, is of interest, but towards London, hidden in modern housing on Green Lane, is Benfleet Hall (formerly Fairmile), Philip Webb's second house (1860) containing a fireplace by W. de Morgan. Across Gwilt's other Cobham bridge, carrying the Portsmouth Road W over the Mole, is Painshill Park which contains a large white late 18th-century house well set above the river. The Park itself was a landmark in the history of landscape architecture. Its grounds were laid out in mid-18th century in the then new picturesque manner by Charles Hamilton complete with a Gothic "abbey" in brick, a Gothic temple (by Batty Langley), cliffs and tunnels near the water and a "hermitage" complete with hermit. These were much admired by Horace Walpole and many others. The four-storey brick folly tower at the W end of the large lake in the grounds was built later in the century and a large iron wheel for raising water from the Mole was added early in the 19th. Rhododendrons were first introduced to England here along with much other exotic planting. The grounds have since been subdivided and the landscape fragmented, the site crossed by a "super-grid" line and most of the structures are now missing or decayed. The loss to Surrey is as great as that of the Tudor palaces. To the NW of Painshill is Silvermere, a large house of 1820 with another large ornamental lake and W of that is Foxwarren Park (1860) by Charles Buxton

Clandon Park, **West Clandon**. Artari ceiling △   and Rysbrack overmantel ▷

and F. Barnes with stepped gables and diapered many-coloured brickwork. Its farm with barge-boarded and stepped gables is one of the most angular buildings in the county.

Coldharbour [8] A small village resting in the high saddle between Coldharbour Common and the outlying Anstiebury Hill with its late Iron Age fort. The village is mainly sandstone cottages strung along the road to Leith Hill with one group facing S to a magnificent view, over the Weald 400 feet below, 20 miles to the South Downs. Christ Church just beyond this is a stone chapel by B. Ferrey (1843).

Collier's Wood* [3] Part of Old Merton on the Wandsworth boundary. Christ Church is by Messrs Francis (1872).

Compton [7] An attractive village of well-tended cottages in small sandstone hills S of the Hog's Back.

The church of St Nicholas, on a little knoll screened by trees from the Street below, is one of the most interesting in Surrey. Much of the body dates from the 11th century and details date from pre-conquest days. The early 11th-century window on the N was recently unblocked to reveal the original frame and horn pane. But the chief interest is its now-unique two-storey Romanesque sanctuary added to the chancel in the late 12th century. The lower stage is groined and the upper is a distinct chapel separated from the chancel by a 12th-century timber rail of round arches on thin capitals headed with crockets,

some of the earliest woodwork in the county. Fittings include an early 12th-century square-bowl font and Jacobean altar rails, pulpit and chancel screen (now by the tower), one roundel of 13th-century glass (of Virgin and Child) in the lower chancel chapel and a tablet and urn of 1778.

The Watts Chapel, **Compton**

Towards the Hog's Back is Limnerslease, the large half-timbered house built by E. George in 1891 for G. F. Watts the painter (1817–1904). There is a museum of his paintings across the road and, nearer the village in the modern cemetery, the burial chapel designed by his wife in 1896 and carried out in red

◁ **Compton** Church

The Watts Chapel, Compton

Watts himself is buried in the "cloister", also designed by Mrs Watts, at the top of the cemetery, worth exploring for other *art nouveau* memorials.

Coombe* [2] There is no village, only a rich wooded Victorian suburb on the hill S of Richmond Park covered with generous private roads and golf courses. John Galsworthy was born here (1867) and the "Robin Hill" of his *Forsyte Saga* is set on the hill. The large and very private houses of the Victorian era have mostly gone and their grounds been filled with smaller houses of all styles but the area is well covered with trees and shrubs and still quiet, private and expensive. Most old and new building is architecturally indifferent—one is grateful for the trees—but there are a few good modern houses, eg Miramonte in Warren Rise by Maxwell Fry (1937) in his international style, and a group of four small houses in Coombe Hill Road by P. Gwynne (1959), and nearby is Cedar Court, a large 15th-century timber-framed house, supposed to have been given to Anne of Cleves, brought here from Colchester in 1910.

Coombe Hill supplied the water for the Tudor Palace of Hampton Court and five Tudor brick conduit houses of Wolsey's time still exist. The best-preserved is Gallows Conduit, behind the convent in George Road; the most visible is Coombe Conduit in Coombe Lane.

Coulsdon* [6] High downland hidden by fairly solid suburbia, with scrubby open spaces to the E. Farthing Downs to the SE is more open and shows traces of Romano–British fields and fourteen barrows, remains of a larger 6th-century cemetery. The

brick with symbolic decoration of Celtic forms in terra-cotta by villagers under her direction. The inside is in a later, *art nouveau*, style covered with gesso in a pattern of ornately framed, elongated angels in dark reds, dark greens and dull gold writhing over its surface. One of the most unexpected interiors in the

The Watts Chapel, interior ▷

church of St John stands on the E side of a well-kept green, unrestored, largely 13th century, with a 15th-century W tower of stone and flint, capped by a later pyramid-and-spike, with shingled roof. There is blank arcading on N and S sides of the old chancel and richly moulded sedilia and piscina. But the old church is now only the anteroom to a much bigger, purply brick nave and sanctuary added on the S side by J. S. Comper in 1958.

Cranleigh [8] The name was changed from "Cranley" to avoid confusion with Crawley, Sussex, in the 19th century. An overgrown village with few good buildings but not unattractive. The best approach is from Guildford across the tapering common through a formal tree avenue into the shopping centre. St Nicholas Church, near the S end, is Wealden cruciform, mainly Decorated, early 14th century. The warm-brown heavily buttressed W tower exhibits put-log holes (left by the scaffolding used in its construction) and is capped by a shingled roof. W. Butterfield restored it in 1864, extending the transepts and adding the S porch. The interior has high wide arcades and tower and chancel arches but outside the tower the feeling of antiquity went with the Butterfield restoration. There is a simple 15th-century screen to the S transept (once the chapel of Baynards, the great house to the S), a 14th-century font with octagonal stem, a late 16th-century lectern and a dripstone in the form of a grinning cat's head.

The cottage hospital near the church, perhaps the first of its kind, occupies a 16th-century building, part half-timbered.

Cranleigh School, a public school founded as the Surrey County School for farmers' sons

and opened in 1865, occupies a Tudor style quadrangle by Woodyer in parkland on rising ground north of the town. Tidy dull neo-Georgian Hall and other buildings were added by Edwin Cooper in 1929. It still has its own farm.

The ground rises steadily N of the school to the steep scarp of the greensand range. At the foot of the scarp is Alderbrook, an early Norman Shaw house of 1881.

SE in woods off the Rudgwick Road is Vachery Pond, a favourite resort of anglers, almost surrounded by woods. This fed the short-lived Wey and Arun Canal which connected the Thames and the S. The top level of the Canal was always short of water and soon foundered financially. Parts can be seen W of Cranleigh and in the woods W of Alford.

Further along the Rudgwick Road, just in the parish of Ewhurst, is Baynards Park, a house of historic but little architectural interest. Built by Sir George More of Loseley at the end of the 16th century as a brick version of that house, it was altered inside and out by M. D. Wyatt in the early 19th century. The exterior in a Tudor style looks attractively picturesque in its parkland setting only at a distance, eg from the road. (Two mile-long tree avenues stretch southward, one of beech, the other of Wellingtonias.)

Crowhurst [9] Gently rolling heavy Wealden-clay land near the Kent boundary, with views of the Downs to the N and the beginnings of Ashdown Forest to the SE. There is no real village. Crowhurst Lane End is a late-Victorian hamlet in Tandridge parish.

The parish church of St George is a simple, comparatively unrestored, building with Wealden

sandstone walls, largely of the late 12th century, but with 13th- and 14th-century windows, a Horsham-slate roof and a sharply spired 15th-century belfry carried on timber framing. In the chancel are the 15th-century table-tombs with brasses to Gaynesfords of Crowhurst Place and on the floor in front of the altar a Wealden cast-iron tomb-slab, the sole example in a Surrey church, to Anne Forster, heiress of the Gaynesfords (d 1591). Outside it is a gigantic yew, perhaps 1,000 years old, which was hollowed out in 1820 to make a room with benches and a padlocked door, now in bad condition. Opposite is Mansion House Farm, a late medieval manor house given a Dutch-style brick W front in the 17th-century while to the S is Crowhurst Place, the moated home of the Gaynesford family from the early 14th to the 18th centuries. The remnants were restored and greatly extended in the early 20th century by George Crawley (who also extended Old Surrey Hall, near Dormansland), when he added new Tudor elevations, chimneys, porch and large additions to N and S, a circular stone dovecote and a half-timbered gatehouse on the Lingfield road. It is now difficult to disentangle old from new but it seems that only the 15th-century hall with its double hammer-beam roof and its immediately adjoining rooms belong to the early house.

Croydon * [6] The most successful shopping and office centre in southern England outside central London and the largest town in Surrey, Croydon is now the nucleus of a London Borough stretching from Coulsdon to Upper Norwood. Although "full of citizens from London" as it was even in Defoe's time, it remains a vigorous provincial town, and has acquired a new character with the large-scale rebuilding of the office and shopping centre in the last fifteen years.

It was an important seat of the Archbishops of Canterbury from the 11th to 19th centuries, a large medieval market (specialising in sheep and walnuts) and an early industrial and communications centre. The Roman road to Lewes went through its centre before turning off at Purley, and this route, continued S of Purley by the 18th-century turnpike which was the first direct Croydon road to Brighton, is still the line of Croydon's High Street and the spine from which important downland valley routes diverge.

Railways followed the turnpike to Croydon. The Surrey Iron Railway, the first public goods railway in the world, was opened from here to Wandsworth in 1803 and extended S to Merstham in 1805. Its toll house, a small cottage in Waddon New Road, can claim to be the earliest ticket office known. A passenger train service from West Croydon to London Bridge started in 1841 some time before other Surrey services. The population rose rapidly from under 6,000 in 1801 to 20,000 by mid-century and over 100,000 by 1891, when Croydon joined London to the N, and its southwards spread along the downland valleys was only checked by recent Green Belt controls.

The town centre moved progressively eastward to follow the N–S communication line, from parish church to High Street, High Street to new office development near East Croydon Station, but recently the through-road route has set up a counter pattern. A by-pass has taken it W of the town since the 1920's and the Crawley motorway will take it still further W.

The early medieval centre was a damp hollow near a source of the Wandle. Here the Archbishops of Canterbury built their palace next to the parish church, and here, surrounded by large areas of pavement and asphalt road where once there was water, both can still be seen. Old Town today is no longer damp, but it has about it an air of mild insecurity as though surprised by its lack of favour in contrast with the bustling High Street only a quarter of a mile away. The Church of St John the Baptist was founded in the 10th century, rebuilt in a perpendicular style in the 15th, and almost destroyed by fire in 1867. The damaged 124 ft tower and the two-storey southern porch were saved and Sir George Gilbert Scott rebuilt the rest to the old plan and style. Outside it looks the big, restored, medieval church which it was before the fire, but inside it looks the Victorian town church with its free use of expensive materials which it really is. Its size, which is large as medieval Surrey churches go, is due to the patronage of the Archbishops, six of whom were buried here. Tombs of Whitgift (d 1604), founder of many charities in the town, and Sheldon (d 1677), benefactor of Oxford, with a white marble effigy, survive. A portrait tablet in the N aisle is to John Singleton Copley, the American artist, who died here in 1815. The 16th-century brass lectern, two 16th-century brasses, fragments of the tomb of Archbishop Grindall, and a 15th-century stoup are also relics of the old church.

The Palace abuts the E end of the churchyard and once almost surrounded it. It was used by the Archbishops of Canterbury before they acquired Lambeth, was popular as a summer retreat and served as head office for their Home Counties estates. Not all liked it; in winter it was dark and damp, being surrounded with trees until the 18th century and water until the 19th. The Archbishops sold it in 1780, having then acquired Addington Palace, and for a century it fell into disuse or served as a factory and laundry. Since 1887 it has been slowly restored to some dignity as a girls' school. It is still the most interesting building in Croydon. The major buildings are packed round two small quadrangles. Most important is the Great Hall, built in the 1380's and rebuilt in 1443–52, of flint rubble with ashlar buttresses, 56 feet long and 38 feet wide, spanned by a medieval roof with moulded beams. Other main rooms are at first-floor level: the 15th-century chapel with 15th- and 17th-century stalls and 17th-century altar rails, the early 14th-century guard room, used as the principal reception room, the dining room, library and 16th-century long gallery.

A quarter-mile E, at the top of Crown Hill, is the centre to which the town had moved by the end of the middle ages. Its atmosphere, however, excepting the historic street market of Surrey Street, is predominantly that of the 1890's, the period when a proud new county borough swept away its central shambles, coaching inns and Georgian slums and rebuilt with commercial blocks, ornate shops and solid theatres. The Town Hall of 1896, a neo-North-German-Renaissance building, with a tall tower to one side, designed by the local architect Charles Henman jr., is a monument to this epoch. Here, at the junction of North End and George Street, is the only other pre-Stuart building of importance. It is a brick-built quadrangle of two-storeyed almshouses with three large gables to North End, looking like a little lost Cambridge college, the Whitgift Hospital founded by that Archbishop in 1596. Its chapel has original backless benches.

New Croydon starts abruptly beyond the Hospital: the twenty-two-storey block of Rothschild House that towers over it from the "Whitgift Centre" is on the site of the grammar school that was Whitgift's other foundation. New office blocks have been built in large parts of central Croydon, some in the older parts, like suckers from new Croydon, but most in the NE quarter near East Croydon Station, because the latter is only 15 minutes' journey from central London. The land available here after World War II gave the Council the opportunity to build a new city. Several million square feet of office space, many thousand square feet of new shopping, public buildings, multi-storey car parks and a new ring road have been built within 15 years. It is sad that in this exciting new building there is so little which is architecturally good and in its planning so little net advantage for either pedestrian or motorist.

New buildings seem to have little plan and the town plan little unity; the seemly buildings are dull and the interesting ones, usually, vulgar. The happiest is probably the Whitgift Centre, mentioned above, where two interlocking pedestrian squares provide the most popular shopping area in the new city. The rest are marred by origami-like concrete frames, green plastic canopies or falling black tiles.

But in Poplar Walk next door to the Whitgift Centre is St Michael's, one of J. L. Pearson's

best churches and perhaps the best building in Croydon. Built 1880–85 and complete except for a projected tower, it is in red brick outside and light brown inside with high, wide, stone-ribbed, vaults, Clayton & Bell glass in the chancel, a jubilee portrait of Queen Victoria in a window at the W end and rich organ case, pulpit and font by G. F. Bodley. The best feature is the view from the narrow ambulatory of the crossing and S chapel. The latter has a little "nave" and "aisles" separated by screens of slim shafts.

To the S, beyond the bad-to-dull civic buildings and the fly-over of 1970 across High Street and brutally jammed in between otherwise acceptable office blocks, is Wrencote, the finest old house in Croydon, early 18th-century red and rubbed brick with gabled wings, pilasters and rich frieze.

Addington, Addiscombe, Norbury, Norwood, Purley, Shirley and Thornton Heath have brief entries of their own but other parts of this large borough are unrewarding. Of some interest is the new building replacing the Church Commissioners' leafy Victorian villas in Park Hill E of the railway, particularly the stepped terraces of St Bernards by the Swiss architects Atelier 5 (1969) and the nearby church for this community, St Matthew, by D. Bush (1971), triangular and appropriately restless.

Cuddington [5] The parish between Ewell and Cheam, now covered with 20th-century housing, whose name almost vanished from the map when the medieval village was razed in 1538 to provide the site for the Tudor palace of Nonsuch, described under Ewell. The church plan and many of the graves were un-

covered in the excavations of the palace in 1959.

Dippenhall [4] A collection of houses on the chalk slopes W of Farnham assembled (1921 on) by Harold Falkner from large parts of 15th, 16th and later centuries half-timbered farm buildings stretched by the architect's fantasy. The best survivor is Overdeans Court of 1930 on the Hampshire border, made from two barns.

Dockenfield [7] A young and formless village on the eastern edge of Alice Holt Forest, transferred from Hampshire in 1895. The church of the Good Shepherd by W. Curtis Green (1910) has Burgate stone walls and brick dressings. The only other building of interest is the Old House, towards Frensham near a pretty reach of the Wey, of the 16th century with 17th-century brick refacing and disused oasthouses all converted to one house.

Dorking [5] Once famous for its medieval poultry market, its breed of five-toed chicken, and its air "esteemed the sweetest in England" as Emanuel Bowen wrote in 1740. In the centre of the best countryside in the county, Dorking is now another London dormitory where every major building of architectural interest, except the church and the White Horse Inn, has been destroyed since World War II. The losses include the two largest houses, Deepdene and Denbies (see Ranmore), as well as Malthus's home at Westcott. What is worse, the buildings which have taken their place are of ingenious banality. Nevertheless the gently reversing horizontal and vertical curves and the raised pavement of the High Street framing view of Box Hill

to E and White Downs to W remain to give the place character.

Stane Street, the Roman road to Chichester, passed through the town by way of a small staging post, but the town has had an uneventful history more marked in fiction than fact. Defoe was at a boarding school here in 1672–6, Disraeli wrote much of Coningsby (1844) at Deepdene, the carved-brick former King's Head at the corner of North Street was the model for the Pickwickian "Marquis of Granby" and the town became temporarily famous following publication in 1871 of Sir George Chesney's account of the conquest of the country by Germans in *The Battle of Dorking*. George Meredith died at Box Hill and is buried in the cemetery, while R. Vaughan Williams (1892–1958) lived many years in the town and created here, with E. M. Forster and others, the annual Leith Hill Festival. The parish church of St Martin is a little N of the High Street and is best seen down surrounding medieval lanes. It is in a sharp 14th-century style by H. Woodyer and is his best work. The body was completed in 1873 and the tower and spire 210 feet high were added in 1874 as a memorial to Bishop Wilberforce ("Soapy Sam"), who died in a riding accident at Abinger that year. The spire is prominent in distant views and makes Dorking the only Surrey town dominated by its church.

There is a handsome brick and stone Italianate Congregational Church in West Street, housing the organ from Brighton Pavilion, on the site of the oldest non-conformist church in the county (1662), and, in Pixham Lane E of the town, is a little neo-Byzantine church by E. Lutyens (1903). The best remaining groups of buildings are the medieval houses and shops in West Street and South Street near their junction with High Street, and the Italianate and neo-Tudor houses in Rose Hill spread round a pretty green approached from South Street by a mock Tudor arch.

S of High Street is another hilly open space, Cotmandene, which was a home of cricket in early 18th century and bred Caffyn, who took the game to Australia, and Jupp. East of here and across the by-pass is Deepdene, whose gardens were compared by John Aubrey with the "kingdome of heaven". The house became best known following its rebuilding by the art collector Thomas ("Athanasius") Hope, a talented designer and first patron of the sculptor Thorvaldsen. His house, badly used by British Rail during World War II, was demolished in 1968 and replaced by a simple modern office block by Scherrer and Hicks. The Dene itself, rampant with rhododendrons, still survives at its rear.

Near Lutyens' little church is the attractive Pixham Mill while the better known Castle Mill is on the Mole and little further E.

On the way back to the town centre past the council offices in "Pippbrook", a crude house by G. G. Scott (1856), the only feature of note is the gabled and half-timbered White Horse Hotel of many centuries, property of Knights Hospitallers in 1278. Outside was the town's Market Place where a half-timbered market hall stood until early in the 19th century. It would be good to see it back.

Dormans Park [9] Following the railway (1884), pleasant Victorian, Edwardian and some good modern houses in wide gravel roads spread prettily in trees to make a first-class Surrey suburb.

To the SE near the Sussex border is Old Surrey Hall, another 15th-century hall-house transformed by George Crawley in the 1920s (cf Crowhurst). His additions to make a quadrangle of mixed timber, brick and stone buildings and a moat round the whole, make it difficult (as at Crowhurst) to untangle old and new but the hall's fascinating roof of scissor rafters and enormous tie beams and the W oriel are genuine relics of the 15th century. The east oriel and the minstrels' gallery are not. These and almost everything else are splendid additions by Crawley; only the addition of a southern wing in a classical stone pattern by W. Godfrey (1927) seems incongruous.

The group is now in divided ownership and the grandeur of Crawley's unity is evaporating.

Lullenden, not far away, has another 15th-century hall range, much restored. Dry Hill in the SE corner of Surrey and the only high point in this part, is an outlier of Ashdown Forest. It is capped by an Iron Age fort buried in woodland.

Dormansland [9] Mainly small cottages of the 19th century on a St Andrew's-cross pattern of roads SE of Lingfield. The indifferent church (St John) is by A. Blomfield (1883).

Dunsfold [7] Brick and tile-hung houses strung along the W side of a long shaggy green with views closed to the N by Hascombe Hill but more open to the heavier Weald on the S.

The church of St Mary and All Saints beside a few old cottages and the old rectory lies half a mile W of the Green down a private-looking road and is approached through tunnels of clipped yew. It is of 1270–90 almost unaltered and though

Dunsfold

modest is perhaps the best Decorated church in Surrey. Only the 15th-century shingled belfry, the heightened chancel arch and the 19th-century vestry are later. Inside are its original fittings: the pews with plain bench-ends surmounted by twin whorls, the double piscina and sedilia with circular shafts and trefoil heads and the font (with 17th-century cover). The timber porch renewed in the 16th century shelters the original ironwork-decorated door.

The Old Rectory is a 15th-century timber-framed building. By the infant Arun is a modern timber shrine by A. D. Caröe (1933) over a Holy Well whose chlorine-rich water is said to cure eye troubles.

Burningfold Manor Farm a mile S of the Green has a massive 15th-century timber-frame and 16th-century refronting, with ornamental timbering between tilehung gables.

Eashing [7] A hamlet of mixed sandstone and timber-framed houses along the lane crossing the Wey above Godalming, best known for its two 13th-century stone rubble bridges over the channels of the Wey. These are

Royal Holloway College, Egham

of four and three arches without
parapet and with cutwaters
pointed upstream and rounded
downstream, a mark of bridges
built by Cisterian monks of

Waverley Abbey.

Their setting forms a popular
picnic and bathing spot, only
jarred by the harsh factory on
the mill site upstream.

East Sheen* [2] East of
"Sheen", the early name for
Richmond. Quiet meandering
roads between the busy
Richmond–Putney road and

from flinty and chalk woodlands on the Downs to heavy clay commons. The old village is spread near the spring line round a square pattern of streets north of the main Guildford road but there are unattractive 20th-century tentacles in all directions and a large suburban blob S of the main road on the chalk.

The church of St Laurence has lost its historic and aesthetic interest from over-restoration but retains in its large mid-13th century S transept and chancel windows, repaired by order of William of Wykeham following neglect by Merton Priory, some original character. The flint-faced W tower is by W. J. Shearburn, 1888.

There is a neat Roman Catholic Church not far NE in an Early English style by E. Bonner, 1913, which now looks older than St Laurence.

The first Lord Howard of Effingham (father of Drake's CO) took his title from the manor held by his family from 1550 to 1647.

The largest building here is the Unigate depot in the Street, an aircraft-type hangar, with offices set with crazy-spaced windows in the end-elevation by R. V. Chellis (1957).

Egham [1] The old Exeter road still winds across the gravelly plain from Staines Bridge, past the historic meadow of Runnymede, through the battered High Street and on up Egham Hill. The Surrey bridgehead though historically important is lacking in visual interest except for the huddle of inns and cottages near Staines Bridge and the 200 foot gasholder not far away.

The church of St John the Baptist is today a sort of bollard for the one-way traffic system imposed on the town centre and its

Richmond Park. Pleasant mid-18th and early 19th-century houses, eg Percy Lodge in Christ Church Road, remain. Christ Church of stone with a SE tower is by Blomfield (1864).

Effingham [5] Another of the long parishes between Guildford and Leatherhead which slope

standardised new shops. It is a Georgian preaching-box built by Henry Rhodes in 1817–20 with squat nave, short chancel and dumpy W tower capped by oval cupola reminiscent of Soane's art gallery at Dulwich, wildly unfashionable until its restoration after fire in 1949 and now bright, well-kept and used. A Virgin and Child by H. Feibusch of 1951 replaces an earlier version damaged by fire. There is a 15th-century timber porch, now used as a lych gate, and inside a splendid royal coat of arms of 1660 and monuments which include an Elizabethan brass of 1576, an alabaster bust of Sir Robert Foster (1663), Lord Chief Justice, of Great Fosters and on staircases to the West Gallery the Denham monuments. One has lifelike portrait reliefs of the two wives of Sir John Denham, Chief Baron of the Exchequer under James I; Lady Eleanor holds in her arms her eldest son the poet, and the other shows Sir John (d 1638) rising shrouded from his grave above a collection of skeletons in high relief. Also in the High Street are the 17th-century brick Red Lion and the neat modern council offices by D. Clarke-Hall (1964).

Beyond, at the top of Egham hill, is the huge, glowing-red, Renaissance "chateau" of the Royal Holloway College, founded by Thomas Holloway (1799–1884) the patent pill millionaire along with the Holloway Sanatorium near Virginia Water. It was modelled on Chambord but in the form of a double quadrangle 550 feet long and 376 feet wide, ie much larger than Hampton Court, by W. H. Crosland, built in 1879–86 and decorated with numerous turrets and with statues which include Gleichen's giant Queen Victoria in the N quad and Mr and Mrs Holloway in the S. The picture gallery contains paintings by eminent Victorians which include Frith's "Railway Station", two late Millais and a Turner. It was one of the earliest women's colleges but has recently been made open to men. Recent buildings in the spacious grounds include curved slabs of residence by Sir Leslie Martin and the more delicate science buildings by Colquhoun & Miller and Michael Brawne.

In the field of Runnymede on the edge of the Thames, Magna Carta was signed by King John in June 1215. It is now a picnic and boating spot, National Trust owned. The road has, at each end, pavilions by E. Lutyens (1929) who also designed the bridge carrying the Staines By-pass over the Thames which was not completed until 1960. Overlooking these is Cooper's Hill, subject of Denham's best-known poem (1642), and, on its edge, the cenotaph to 20,000 Commonwealth airmen designed as a cloister with viewing tower by E. Maufe (opened 1953). It has good views but ironically too many aircraft for comfort. Nearby is the J. F. Kennedy memorial, a stone block of impressive simplicity by G. A. Jellicoe.

To the S of the town is the large 16th-century brick house Great Fosters named after Robert Foster (see above), its best known occupant, now a hotel. Flat projecting tops of two staircase towers give it an impressive silhouette.

Ellen's Green [8] A hamlet in the Weald near the Sussex border SE of Cranleigh with half-timbered houses scattered round a green.

Elstead [7]. An over-enlarged village between Wey meadows and heaths that stretch 3 miles SW to Thursley and Churt. The old village marked by mixed sandstone, brick and tile-hung cottages is centred on a small triangular green from which the Farnham Road winds down to the medieval 5-arched stone bridge over the Wey. Another of the Waverley pattern with rounded cut-waters downstream and marred, like Tilford, by a modern bridge close by.

In the flat meadows beyond are the most attractive buildings in the parish, the 4-storey 18c mill, in red brick with a little Palladian cupola, and the linked 2-storey mill house.

The church of St James, tucked away down a lane SW of the green is a relative disappointment. It has 13c walls and later fragments, notably the graceful 15c E window, but these were stuck together with a new south aisle in a ruthless restoration of 1871 which has made the church, with the exception of the western timber bellcote, an almost characterless whole. 19c and 20c expansion of the village to the south onto Pot and Elstead Commons and then in larger lumps along the Milford road to the east was followed by more controlled, but not prettier, infilling and made the village into another Surrey suburb with restaurants and poodle parlours. Time and trees are now healing the worst aesthetic sores.

North of the Wey on a little wooded hill is Fulbrook, a Lutyens house of 1897 in a near-Tudor style but amalgamating rubble walls, large brick chimneys, weather boarding and tile hanging with semi-classical interiors. The whole was redeemed by the Jekyll garden and a little chimney-dominated lodge.

Englefield Green [1] West of Cooper's Hill and now a suburb of Egham, though it still gives the impression of a separate hamlet of low buildings scattered round a green on the edge of Windsor Park. The church, St Simon and St Jude, by E. B. Lamb (1859) is lined internally with colourful bands of brick and stone.

Epsom [5] Home of Epsom Salts and the Derby, and one of the larger Surrey towns, joined insolubly to the SW suburbs of London, for which it has been a popular dormitory since the 18th century. The early village grew up along Church Street, E of the present shopping centre and close to the Roman Stane Street, but spread W along the present High Street after the discovery of the "old" well on the Common in 1618. The water was rich in "Epsom salts" (hepta-hydrated sulphate of magnesium) and became a popular cure for many ailments including indigestion. The well now stands locked in two sets of iron railings and surrounded by bungalows of Epsom Wells Estate, isolated itself by the common.

The village was a popular resort by the Restoration and an account of a gay visit (in 1667) is in Pepys' *Diary*. Many hotels were built in this period, though few are left. Waterloo House in the High Street was formerly the New Inn and had one of the earliest assembly rooms in the country. The first daily post from London was to Epsom (1684). A new well was opened in 1707 behind the Old Manor House (not far W of the New Inn) and nearer to the High Street than the old well and this, under its energetic proprietor Livingstone, became more popular than the old. The Old Well fell into disuse as a consequence (and not through any malice of Livingstone, *pace* most local histories) but the New Well itself depended on the management of its owner and after Living-

stone's death (1727) the Spa collapsed and the New Well too was closed. No sign is left today.

Luckily the town's popularity as a summer residence and that of its Downs for running horses was growing. The fillies' race named the Oaks, after the Earl of Derby's house at Carshalton, was founded in 1779, and the Derby, for colts and fillies, in 1780.

The town has grown continuously and almost all the surrounding land, except ancient commons and racing establishments near the Downs, is now covered with houses.

The parish church of St Martin in Church Street, which runs SE from the High Street, still retaining a few early 18th and 19th-century houses in its toothy length, is an ungainly building with 15th-century tower, flint and stucco nave built in 1825, and an E end and transepts begun in 1908 by C. Nicholson as part of a larger, unfinished, rebuilding in brown stone with some flint. In the chancel are monuments by Flaxman, Chantrey and John Bacon jnr. The font is a simple late 15th-century octagon and the church has a copy of the "Vinegar" Bible (1717).

Just E stood (until 1967) Pitt Place, the principal house of the old town, home of Lyttletons and later of Mrs Fitzherbert.

The High Street itself is Surrey neo-Georgian inter-war shopping parade, E of Ashley Road, but westwards is more interesting. Most of the 18th-century spa-life was centred here, and this still is its Market Place. It retains some character though most of the earlier buildings have gone. The best is Waterloo House. The Clock Tower, with lavatories at the base, is of 1848 and replaces an old Watch Tower.

Epsom is rich in Georgian houses, but those in the centre

have gone and the rest are scattered. In Church Street the best are The Cedars and Ebbisham House. The rest are largely in the Woodcote area and they include Woodcote End House, Westgate House (gutted internally), Woodcote Green House, Woodcote Grove (crowded with office buildings) and Durdans of 1764–8, by W. Newton but much altered in the 19th century, the home of the fifth Earl of Rosebery from 1847–1929. Parts of Nonsuch Palace (see Ewell) were used in its foundation and the fine wrought-iron gates to Chalk Lane were brought here from Chandos, Middlesex. Finest of all is Woodcote Park near the R.A.C. Country Club, originally built for Richard Evelyn, brother of the diarist, in the 17th century and rebuilt in stone for Lord Baltimore. One of its rooms in a French rococo style is preserved in Boston, U.S.A., but most were destroyed by fire in 1934 leaving only the base of Baltimore's house. The E front is a copy in brick of the 18th-century brick and stone.

South-east of the town is Epsom College, originally the Royal Medical Benevolent College, founded in 1853.

Ashley Road rises southward from the central cross roads, past the new School of Art with its white concrete frame and dark facing bricks by R. Ash (County Architect), 1969–71, to the racecourse, with its grandstand, an ugly early concrete structure of 1927, and fine views S over chalk countryside. The best walk is from Woodcote to the Downs up Chalk Lane between racing stables and exercise fields.

N of the town is a group of mental hospitals for several thousand patients settled by the London County Council about 1900.

Esher [5] A pleasant town on

Esher Old Church

three little hills, divided by the overloaded Portsmouth Road (now being by-passed), surrounded by expensive wooded suburbs and separated from built-up London and neighbouring "villages" by an unparalleled ring of open spaces: Sandown Park racecourse to the N, Littleworth and Arbrook Commons to the E, Esher Common to the S and West End Common and the flood plain of the Mole to the W.

The old church of St George's, with a Tudor body in chequered golden sandstone and 18th- and 19th-century additions in dun-red brick and a timber belfry, is S of the High Street behind the Bear Inn. It was superseded by the large new church to the N in 1854 and thereby spared from later restorations. The brick chapel on the S side of the old church was added in 1725–6 by Vanbrugh as a family pew for the Duke of Newcastle, then owner of Claremont (*v. inf*). It has Corinthian pillars facing the nave like a little temple. Queen Victoria often worshipped here. There are monuments to Lady Fowler (d 1738) by Henry Cheere, to Princess Charlotte (d 1817), previously at Claremont which shows her husband Prince Leopold accepting the Belgian crown with Britannia's approval, and to Georgina Ellis (d 1820) by Flaxman.

The newer parish church of Christ Church is by Ferrey (1854), of stone with a broach spire in a 13th-century style. It dominates the green N of the High Street. It contains a monument to Sir Richard Drake (1603) brought from St George's and a marble effigy of Leopold of the Belgians (1867) by Susan Durant. The E Window is by N. Comper.

The High Street is mainly neo-Tudor and neo-Georgian shops but the local Council offices are in a tall late 17th-century house, much altered but containing an elegant early 18th-century staircase.

Opposite is the racecourse of Sandown Park, the site of Sandon Hospital which was founded in the 12th century and amalgamated with St Thomas's Hospital (London) in 1436. Its 1973 grandstand with huge cantilevered roof was designed by Fitzroy Robinson.

On the Green there are old cottages sheltered by Sandown's wooded hill and the lodges of the Esher Place estate. Here was the extensive house of Bishop Wayneflete of Winchester but all that remains is the three-storey gatehouse of red brick diapered with blue which stands by the river Mole, crowded with Tudor-style 20th-century houses. This was made picturesque in rococo Gothic style by William Kent for the younger brother of the Duke of Newcastle of Claremont. The large house in the centre of the estate is a much newer French-style Esher Place, by Robinson and Duchène (1898) with a sunk garden by E. Lutyens (1905).

Claremont lies to the S where Sir John Vanbrugh built a "romantick" crenellated house and walled gardens which he sold to Thomas Pelham, later Duke of Newcastle. Pelham had the house enlarged by Vanbrugh and gardens laid out by William Kent with a lake, enclosing an islanded temple, and a grotto. Lord Clive bought the estate in 1768, pulled down Vanbrugh's house (though the walled garden and gazebo remain) and employed Lancelot Brown and Henry Holland to design a smaller house. This is a dignified Palladian box on a small rise, in white brick with stone dressings and a giant portico with Corinthian columns. It has an entrance hall with red scagliola columns and oval ceiling, and a great drawing-room with ornamented attractive plaster ceiling. Brown altered and extended the gardens to the S and E but left most of Kent's work alone. The estate was bought in 1816 for Princess Charlotte, only child of George IV, and Leopold, later first King of the Belgians. Charlotte died here in childbirth in 1817 but Leopold stayed on till 1831 and was much visited by his niece Victoria. It became the home of the French Imperial family and both Louis Philippe and his queen died here (1850 and 1866). Queen Victoria acquired it in 1882.

The estate was broken up in the 1920s; much of the E side was developed for housing of the expensive Surrey type; the house with part of the Brown landscape became a girls' school and the western part by Kent, now somewhat overripe, was acquired by the National Trust.

Ewell [5] A tiny town of twisted roads around pools at the source of the Hog's Mill River, much loved by pre-Raphaelite painters. Holman Hunt painted his "Hireling Shepherd" and John Millais his "Death of Ophelia" here. The focus and most important building was Bourne Hall, set behind the Talbot-crowned arch in the main street, but this was replaced in 1970 by a circular library and social centre by Sheppard Fidler in brick and concrete, rather too large for its delicate setting. A lake survives.

The church of St Mary is round a bend not far away, an indifferent building by Henry Clutton, 1848, with 15th-century screen, font and memorials from the medieval old church. The latter's 15th-century tower still stands in pleasing decay in the graveyard to the S overlooking the grave of James Lowe (1866), one of those credited with the invention of the screw-propeller. There are medieval houses, converted to shops, in the centre but the best are tucked away in Church Street S of the old church.

There is an early 18th-century mill, down-stream from Bourne House in a pleasant open space along Kingston Road.

Just across the Ewell By-pass is the low overgrown brick base of the Tudor banqueting house built as an adjunct to Nonsuch Palace, while between Ewell and Cheam is Nonsuch Park, the home park of the great palace begun by Henry VIII with the ruthless destruction in 1538 of the parish church and manor house of Cuddington to make its site. Stone from the dispossessed Merton Priory provided the foundations. It was intended to outshine Wolsey's Hampton Court and the contemporary extravagances of Francis I and was sensational in its time. Arranged around two courtyards nearly twice the size of Wolsey's palace it was the principal building work of Henry VIII's lifetime though he did not live to see it completed. The courtyards were flanked by gatehouses and two great octagonal towers which swelled out in their second storeys on heavy corbels. The ground floor was of stone but above that was timber-framed; this frame was covered with slate while between the timbers the walls were plastered and decorated with figures in high relief, like work done for Francis I, in the charge of the Italian master Nicholas Bellin whom Henry had persuaded to leave France. It was completed by the Earl of Arundel, and reverted to Elizabeth I who spent much of her later life here. But it was an extravagant lodge in a hunting estate, not popular with later rulers, and suffered a period of long neglect, save for brief glory during the plague and fire in

London when the Exchequer was moved here.

Charles II returned to England in a ship named "Nonsuch" after his royal estate, but gave the palace to the Countess of Castlemaine in 1669. A large part of the inner court was then taken by its caretaker, Lord Berkeley, to build Durdans at Epsom; and the rest sold for the price of its fittings. Hardly a sign of this enormous house, once the most fascinating and important building in Surrey, remains. It stood S of the present London Road Lodge. Finds from the 1959–60 excavation are in the London Museum.

Ewhurst [8] The Greensand crest of Pitch Hill stares down the main street of this Wealden village, straggling from a small square at the N to a long green on the road S.

The church of Peter and Paul in the centre is built of sandstone with sturdy Norman-style central tower and broach spire by Robert Ebbels (1838). The chancel was rebuilt at the same time but the rest is largely unrestored Norman with later windows. The massive early 12th-century S doorway is the best in Surrey. Inside are a Jacobean pulpit and delicate late 17th-century altar rails from Baynards Park (v. Cranleigh).

The best village houses are Tudor House, with 15th-century herring-bone brick filling between close timber-framing, and Old Cottage, late 17th-century brick and half-timber below and scalloped and straight tilehanging above. On the wooded slopes to the N are a number of late Victorian houses: Con`eyhurst by P. Webb (1886), Woolpit by George and Peto, decorated with terracotta befitting its Doulton owners (1888), and Long Copse by Alfred Powell (1897), of stone part

Entrance to Bourne Hall, **Ewell**

Horsham-slated, part thatched, with interior woodwork by E. Gimson. G. F. Watts, the artist of Compton, thought it the most beautiful house in the country.

It is worth ascending the 843 feet of Pitch Hill (Coneyhurst) for its views over the village and the Weald to the South Downs and on each side along the Greensand escarpment.

Farleigh* [6] There is no village, only St Mary's church and the ugly farm buildings of Farleigh Court, isolated in high chalk country. The tower of Warlingham Park Hospital to the S and the tower-flat tops at New Addington peer over the trees. Otherwise nothing is to be seen but ploughed fields and woods; an amazing survival less than five miles from the centre of Croydon. The church is a simple early Norman room with an extension to the chancel of the late 13th century, when lancet

windows were added to the NE and S, and with a later W porch and bell turret.

Farncombe [7] Once an independent village a mile N of Godalming, it is now largely a 19th–20th century suburb of the latter though it retains old houses in its Street and has its own station and a late 19th-century church by George Gilbert Scott. In the Guildford Road, near Godalming Bridge, are the Wyatt Almshouses built in 1622 in a Tudor Jacobean range of ten dwellings with a central gabled chapel facing the road.

Farnham [7] Dominated by the Bishop's Castle guarding the western entry to Surrey, once the most important corn-market in the county, it is now best known for Georgian houses and associations with William Cobbett. Its backbone is the prehistoric route

Farnham

still followed by West and East Street and from this the more imposing Castle Street runs N to the chalk bluff bearing the Castle, while Downing Street runs S, side-stepping the medieval church to the bridge over the Wey. South Street further E was made after the coming of the railway in 1849.

Mesolithic, Neolithic, Bronze and Iron Age finds have been made in chalk, gravel or sand excavations here and a Roman pottery and bathhouse for its workers were found by the Aldershot road. The manor was granted to Bishops of Winchester in 688 and a castle to guard its growing market was built in early Norman times. Henry of Blois, brother of King Stephen, completed a mound some 30 feet high round the base of a tower in local chalk rock which rose another 60 or 70 feet. Its well, 13 feet square, can be seen at the top of the present

mound but most of the tower was destroyed by order of Henry II in 1155. The whole castle was, however, remodelled largely in its present form later in the century. It took on a steadily more domestic appearance in the 13th century with the formation of the lower domestic court and was then favoured by Bishops and graced by royal visits down to that of George III. The most notable addition was Wayneflete's great entry tower to the domestic court in local brick, 1470–75. This made the first extensive use of material other than chalk, though parts of the chalk had already been replaced and the patchy appearance of the castle today is due to repair of the original rock with varied materials. Wayneflete also extended the keep by building a shell wall outside Henry's earth mound, filling in the gap and adding domestic corner towers. The castle

was on the frontier of Parliament-held territory in the Civil War and changed hands several times (the opposing poets George Wither and John Denham each held it for a time) and it was slighted under the Commonwealth. Repairs and additions were made at the Restoration by Bishop Morley, who built the grand staircase and refitted the chapel. Following the transfer in 1927 to the new diocese of Guildford, its domestic part was converted to a conference centre and retreat and the keep taken into state guardianship.

The parish church of St Andrew lies S of West Street near the river. It is a large rather plain building with a massive polygonally-buttressed, 15th-century W Tower (with pinnacles by E. Christian 1865) dominating the water meadows. The nave and aisles are of similar height which with the drastic restoration of B.

Ferrey, 1841–5, have given the interior a slightly lifeless look. There are Norman fragments—eg corbels in the chancel; chapels were added about 1200 and most of the rest is mid-14th century though the chancel was lengthened at the end of the 14th. The piscina and sedilia are delicately detailed 15th century, the octagonal font is 15th and the altar rails late 17th century. The weakly-coloured E window is by A. W. N. Pugin. A statue of St Andrew in the S chapel is by Eric Gill and at the W end is a monument with a medallion portrait by J. H. Foley to Cobbett and a timidly-lettered plaque by Gill to George Sturt (see Bourne). Cobbett is buried outside the N door beneath a marbled altar tomb beside the simple stone slab to his father.

Other Farnham churches are disappointing. St James in East Street is in poor Gothic by H. Woodyer (1876) while the Roman Catholic Church of St Joan of Arc is in neo-Georgian brick of 1930. It contains a few carved stones from Waverley Abbey. The best streets are Castle Street and West Street. The former is a picture postcard view of an English town of triumphantly diverse buildings. The best individual houses, the late 18th-century Palladian Castle Hill House and Guildford House are at the top and the Windsor Almshouses, built 1619 for "eight poor, honest old impotent persons" now look small and shabby among expensive neighbours lower down. At the foot of Castle Street where once stood an attractive half-timbered market hall, the Borough links West and East Streets. It has some medieval features such as the courtyard behind Borelli's but is chiefly interesting for its pre-Georgian and neo-Georgian buildings.

The Town Hall is by the local architect Harold Falkner, built 1930–4 to replace a crude Victorian building and to bring the corner into harmony with Castle Street. Falkner joined this to the Bailiffs Hall (1674), rebuilding it with intricate niches and gables but leaving the Jacobean baroque on the East side, and next door he rebuilt a neo-Tudor bank by Norman Shaw in his own neo-Georgian, leaving one of Shaw's chimneys rising above the Bailiffs Hall.

In West Street a long line of fine houses has suffered from the spread of shops and shop windows and the best remaining are away from the Borough. In Vernon House, a 16th-century building rebuilt in 1727, Charles I stayed on his last journey to London. Willmer House in baroque brickwork of 1718 has the finest cut-brick facade in the country and Sandford House is a later somewhat provincial baroque of 1757. Downing Street to its S is more modest pleasant 18th century with little 17th- and 18th-century cottage-lined lanes leading off to the church.

Cobbett's birthplace, now The William Cobbett P.H., then a farmhouse, is across the river while the pleasant late 19th-century Maltings nearby are being converted to communal use.

N of the Castle are two further good houses, the handsome brick Grange of 1710 to its NW and the early 18th-century brick Ranger's House to its NE. The rest of the town has suffered badly from replacement and infilling with indifferent to bad neo-Georgian buildings. The only good modern building is the large new School of Art in the Hart, W of Castle Street, by the County Architect, R. Ash, of which the first stage was opened in 1969.

Fetcham [5] Sprawling, mainly interwar, housing reaching from Leatherhead to Great Bookham, following the common pattern of villages from Croydon to Guildford, with the more expensive properties on chalk to the S, a medieval village on the spring line in the middle, sloping to clay commons and denser development to the N.

The church of St Mary, still pleasantly screened by trees from the surrounding road at the SE corner of the old village, has a pre-Conquest origin, showing Roman brick dressing above the S arcade. This and the tower's base are 11th century, while the chancel, N transept and N aisle are much altered early 13th century. The tower was completed in 18th-century brick and flint. Just E is Fetcham Park, a large house of brick and stone built by William Talman about 1716 but so encrusted with French classical style embellishments in 1870 as to be unrecognisable. The main feature of the much-altered interior is the early 18th-century staircase with carved balusters and walls and ceilings painted by Laguerre, while its park is covered with arch neo-Georgian cottages.

Development SE of Fetcham Park is interesting for its bad layout, many plots being ten times deeper than their width, so that back gardens end out of sight in an impenetrable jungle.

To the N The Street is still nicely villagey as far as the much-altered Old Rising Sun public house which incorporates a 15th-century stone hall with kingpost roof.

Frensham [7] Known for its ponds, the largest in Surrey, on the wide sandy heath S of Farnham. There is scattered development in three clusters, at Millbridge on the main road to the NE, along the lane past the church, and at Spreakley to the

Friday Street

NW. The few interesting buildings are scattered.

The Church of St Mary has a massive late 14th-century W tower of sandstone rubble with huge buttresses but is otherwise neo-Decorated by Hähn (1868). Inside is a three-foot-wide copper cauldron popularly associated with a local witch "Mother Lud-lam" and a defaced 13th-century monument with crocketed pin-nacles. On the Wey to the W is the 16th-century timber-framed Frensham Beale Manor with a stone-built chapel. Frensham Heights, a mile NW of Spreakley (and just within the parish of Farnham) is a large brick and stone Tudor-style building of 1900 housing a well-known co-ed school, while at Millbridge on a bluff above the Wey is another school in Pierrepoint, a large house by N. Shaw (1876), half-timbered above the stone ground floor and once decorated inside with leather panels.

The Great Pond is to the S along the Hindhead road, the Little Pond down a lane to the E. The Great Pond is used for sailing, and rowing-boats can be hired on the Little Pond, but both ponds are over-popular at summer week-ends and the vegetation and soft soil round both have been badly damaged by cars. Low sandy heath runs S from the Little Pond to the sharp little sandstone hills, the Devil's Jumps, near Churt.

Friday Street [8] A hamlet, part of the extensive Wotton estate, set in a tight pine-wooded valley on a tributary of the Tilling-bourne here dammed to make a large hammer pond which reflects the popular Stephen Langton pub and the wooded hills. Best not visited on sunny summer week-ends.

Frimley [4] An old village in the Blackwater valley on the Hants border, badly treated in the years since World War II. The atmosphere of country coaching has given way to indifferent shopping parades and the overflow of Camberley and Farnborough. Pine-wooded sandy hills to the E are still pleasant, though much is disappearing under new bungalows, and in places one can obtain wide views of miles of apparently unspoilt country. There were, however, few buildings of interest in Frimley and little has been lost except its pleasant character.

St Peter's church is of stone in a 15th-century style with a small W tower by J. T. Parkinson (1825), replacing an early 17th-century half-timbered church. To the north is Frimley Park, now an Army Training School, a largely late 18th-century house, incorporating a late 17th-century staircase from its predecessor. In its park is a three-storey hospital, prototype for many others by Department of Social Security Architects, built in 1971.

Opposite St Peter's are seven blocks of white-brick houses by Derek Sharp (1969)—probably the best new building here but with an eccentric pattern of semicircular windows.

Frimley Green, one mile S, is quieter and more villagey but going the way of Frimley. It has its own little church in brick and stone 15th-century style by Poulter and Poulter (1911), hidden in trees S of the L.S.W.R. line.

Gatton [6] Scenically, historically and architecturally fascinating. There is no village, simply a church, a large house and landscaped park, set in a fold of the North Downs. It had two members of Parliament from 1450 to 1832 and was one of the most "rotten" of the boroughs swept away by the great Reform Act.

The church of St Andrew is in the middle of the park laid out by Lancelot Brown in 1762; he also designed the park at Upper Gatton on the hilltop. It is basically a dull medieval building with mean windows altered out of recognition in the 1830's for the owner, Lord Monson. The N transept was converted with a fireplace and padded benches into an elaborate family pew for the Monsons and joined to the great house by a covered way. Architectural fragments of other churches were inserted and valuable fittings added—Low Countries glass in the E windows and the best collection of woodwork to be seen in the county, a 15th-century English rood-screen supporting the W gallery, stalls from a large church at Ghent, panelling from Aarschot dated 1515 fitted in the nave, and an early 16th-century pulpit in the S transept. In the Chancel, Burgundian panelling surrounds the church's original 13th-century piscina, the altar rails are Flemish 18th-century work and the altar table is 16th century. (The linen-fold patterned doors in the S transept came from northern France.)

The great house has been rebuilt and altered many times, lastly by Edwin Cooper in 1936, who incorporated the impressive portico of ten Corinthian columns of 1891 from the previous house. N of this is the "Town Hall", a little Doric temple with six iron columns and, in front, a large urn inscribed "Stat Ductis Sortibus Urna" ("the Urn remains when the lots have been drawn") dated 1765, where the members of Parliament were "elected".

Set too close to the Town Hall and occupying much of the northern part of the park are indifferent buildings of the 1950s, housing the Royal Alexandra and Albert School for orphans, founded in 1864.

The southern part with its large lake is largely as planned by Brown and retains its early 19th-century lodges, picturesque thatched on Rocky Lane and breezy Italianate on the Reigate road.

Gatton Bottom, a lovely chalk combe on the N of the Park, leads to the top of Reigate Hill and is followed by the Motorway M25.

Gatwick [9] London's second airport, on the Brighton road. Before the war there was a racecourse at Gatwick Park on the N and an airfield (1936) with a circular control tower and offices on the S. The new airport was not opened without a fight, and arguments then were as numerous and compelling as those against sites for London's third airport. But it was approved by the Government of the day and farmland, racecourse, old airfield, and parts of the village of Lowfield Heath disappeared within it. The old terminal building still stands but divorced from the airport by the diverted Brighton road. The new airport is too close to the new town of Crawley over the Sussex boundary and has made the quiet villages of Charlwood and Burstow noisy; unbearably so at summer weekends. Well-proportioned new buildings of three storeys with glass curtain-walls with exposed steel stanchions outside and concrete columns inside, by Yorke, Rosenberg and Mardell (1958) integrated the passenger terminal with the new railway station on the E side, spanning the Brighton road in the process. The second-stage office block was added in 1968. The airport was transferred to W Sussex in 1974.

Godalming [7] An attractive compact medieval town on the Portsmouth Road four miles from

Guildford in the deep curved valley of the Wey; wooded slopes are the backcloth to all the old streets. Newer suburbs have spoilt much surrounding plateau land but are hidden from the old town. It has for centuries been a centre of the West Surrey woollen manufacture in spite of its rise and fall at Guildford and elsewhere.

The main streets meet at the W end of High Street, where they focus on the Market Hall, a lengthened stucco octagon by John Perry in 1814, now a local museum above open arcades. From its delicate elevation to the High Street, capped by heavy eaves and cupola, it is known locally as the "Pepperpot". The church of Saints Peter and Paul dominates Church Street and many distant views, with its twisted spire, not far N. The tower was built over the Saxon chancel, which was extended E. Transepts were added in the 12th century, the tower was raised and the nave rebuilt in the 13th, and the timber-framed lead-covered spire added in the 14th. The church was much altered in the 19th when aisles and W end were rebuilt and the internal proportions were greatly altered in 1879 by G. G. Scott, who removed the Saxon chancel arch which served as the W arch of the tower and raised the Norman E arch by four feet. The overall effect is now dull but the S chapel's E window with early geometric tracery, and the 13th-century piscina with two aumbries above and the Decorated sedilia in the chancel are worth seeing. The Rev. Owen Manning (d 1801), joint author of Manning and Bray's *History of Surrey* is buried in the churchyard, on the N side of which is Thackeray Turner's memorial cloister of 1913 to J. G. Phillips, wireless operator of the *Titanic*.

A walk downstream brings one past the Lammaslands to the late 18th-century bridge. Return by Bridge Street and High Street along the spine of the town takes one past a busy variety of buildings which include the 18th-century, red and grey brick King's Arms Hotel, the three-storey 17th-century No. 80 High Street in decorative brick patterns and the exposed 16th-century frame of Nos. 99–103. Even better townscape is behind the "Pepperpot" in Church Street with its curves and gay variety, and an office of the Department of Employment sheltering behind Georgian brick and Regency bow-windows more suitable for a tea-shop.

Beyond the station is the 19th-century Meath House on the site where General Oglethorpe, founder of Georgia, was born in 1696.

Commanding the plateau above is Charterhouse School, the public school founded in Finsbury in 1611. It moved here in 1872, to the central mass of buildings with five towers by Philip Hardwick junior. The assembly hall is by A. Blomfield 1885, and the War Memorial Chapel, in a free early-Gothic style, is by Giles Gilbert Scott, 1927. The best modern building is the Art block by G. A. Jellicoe (1958) and this has been spoilt by later extensions. Old Carthusians include Crawshaw, Thackeray, John Wesley, Max Beerbohm (his school reports said "silly") and R. Vaughan Williams ("noisy").

Seven new boarding houses, up to 8 storeys high in orange brick by Adrian Scott 1975 cluster N of playing fields.

Godstone [6] A large village near the foot of the North Downs, chiefly memorable for the big tree-shaded green praised by Cobbett, seen from the Eastbourne Road. Its pond at the SE corner, overhung with chestnut and lime, reflects the fine 16th-century timber frame of the Clayton Arms, the White Hart of Cobbett's *Rural Rides*, across the road. Also on the Eastbourne Road is the Bell Inn, mainly early 18th century but incorporating earlier work.

The church of St Nicholas lies in an almost secret, separate village known as Church Town away from main roads half a mile to the E. Sir Gilbert Scott lived at a gaunt Georgian house to the N called Rooksnest (now Strete Court School) and all but rebuilt the church in 1873. Of the old church there remain Norman window fragments on the W wall, the 15th-century octagonal font and monuments to the Godstone branch of the Evelyn family (see Long Ditton and Wotton). Scott added a S aisle, altered the picturesque SE tower and heightened its shingled spire. The monument to Sir John Evelyn (half-brother to the father of John, the diarist) has recumbent effigies in black marble (1641). A sarsen stone in the churchyard marks the grave of S. F. Miles (1908), one of the earliest organisers of rambling.

To the S are the picturesque timber-framed St Mary's Homes in a free Tudor style by Scott (1872) with flèche-capped chapel, and many gables composing a nice group with the church spire.

Twentieth-century compositions of geometric housing estate and rigid reservoirs (ex glass sand pits) N of the village are less happy.

Gomshall [5] (Pronounced Gumshal.) A village on low sandy hills S of the Downs; a modest version of Shere, about one mile E of it but not as precious, though it hardly deserves the ferocious caravan pitch on its country station's doorstep. The old tannery on the main road is its largest building, acceptably screened by trees and older houses. Alongside is a 16th-century packhorse bridge over the Tillingbourne. Just W on the main-road corner is the early 17th-century, dark-red brick, King John House. S of the railway is the Manor House with an elegant early 18th-century S front, in red and grey brick, with Doric porch and a late 17th-century E end in sandstone. Scattered 19th- and 20th-century houses and even considerable "streets" in the light lands and pine woods to the S. The most interesting house is Burrows Cross by Norman Shaw (1889), unassuming, with tilehung upper floor.

Grafham [8] Hamlet on the Guildford–Horsham road with an apsed chapel dedicated to St Andrew, built by H. Woodyer in 1864. He lived in Grafham Grange, to the W, a rather unattractive house of the same date. The church screen is of wood but part of the structure of the church to obviate the censure of the then Bishop of Winchester, who refused on theological grounds to consecrate churches with screens.

Grayswood [7] A village round a smooth triangular green set in rolling pine woods with glimpses of higher ground near Hindhead to the W. The church of All Saints with its timber bell-turret

The Red House, **Godalming**   **Godalming** Market Hall ▷

is by a Swedish architect Axel Haig (1902), now buried in the churchyard. N of the green is the White House by A. Connell (1932) in the then continental modern style, L-shaped with a glazed staircase in the angle and concrete walls, cantilevered from columns.

Guildford [4] "The prettiest and taken altogether the most agreeable and happy looking town that I saw in my life," said Cobbett. It is still the most agreeable in Surrey. Its castle commanded the gap cut by the river Wey through the chalk downs. It was a borough by 1130, seat of the Assizes from 1256 to 1930 (when they went with the County Council to Kingston). The see of Guildford was created in 1927, and the young University of Surrey moved here from Battersea in the 1960s.

The best entry is along London Road past Peter Shepheard's sober Civic Hall, 1963, to the upper High Street, which starts at the junction of Epsom Road. On the S is the Wren style, brick, Somerset House and then the stone-gabled quadrangle of the Royal Grammar School, 1557–1586. The chained library on the N has a document describing cricket being played here about 1550. Archbishop Abbott, Speaker Onslow and artist John Russell were pupils. Downhill, High Street lurches to the left and starts its steep descent to the Wey between the towers of Holy Trinity Church and Abbott's Hospital while North Street, formerly Lower Backside, slides off first right and then left to parallel High Street. North Street was the site of the cattle market till the late 19th century, retains a thriving street market and the air of a distinct and prosperous Victorian town.

Holy Trinity was rebuilt in brick by J. Horne with a battlemented brick tower by the local architect J. Garton. New chancel and apse were added by A. W. Blomfield in 1888 and the interior gutted to make one open rectangular hall. The 16th-century freestone and flint-chequered Weston Chantry on the S survives only as a vestry. S of the altar is the tomb of Archbishop Abbott (1562–1633), erected by M. and J. Christmas in 1640 with alabaster effigy and spiky canopy and a brass to the Archbishop's parents of 1606, while in the nave is a reclining figure of Speaker Arthur Onslow, buried at Merrow 1778. The churchyard was a pleasant square until the arrival of the concrete convoluted parking garage to the S, which crowds the church and neighbouring 18th-century Guildford Club. Opposite is Abbott's Hospital built 1619–22 by the Archbishop as a home for 20 poor persons. It is a single three-storey quadrangle in red brick with a giant gatehouse more appropriate for a Cambridge college, three stages high with big octagonal-capped corner turrets. The quad itself is modest but the dining room and chapel are worth seeing for the Jacobean fittings and the chapel for the Flemish glass telling the story of Jacob. A few doors down is the late 17th-century Guildford House, whose original doorcase is set between 18th-century bow windows. Its rear has tilehanging disguised as brickwork (once common in the High Street). The staircase has openwork floral panels. A little further is Guildford Old Bank founded 1765 with rococo plasterwork and then the Guildhall, the most notable and attractive building in the street. The present ship-like front (1683) with its heavily projecting bal-

conied and pedimented, first floor, with a great clock projecting on a gilded beam, capped by octagonal cupola, dominates views up and down the street. The ground floor contains the Courtroom with 16th-century ceiling, 18th-century panelling and 17th-century glass, while the upper floor has the Council Chamber with a carved chalk chimney-piece, and the finest municipal regalia in the county.

Across the road is Tunsgate, the massive Tuscan portico of the former Corn Exchange of 1818 now a gateway to a square bright with new shops.

Next is a gabled and bow-windowed building of 1536 and then a run of mixed buildings (including a good early 18th-century front to No. 56) down to the corner of Quarry Street. The more important commercial buildings have concentrated on the right or N side opposite here. Harveys has an early 19th-century front screening the main five-storey block by G. A. Jellicoe. This has a delicate roof garden of pools giving views over old High Street and Quarry Street roofs, but it forms a long squared silhouette that is unattractive when seen from any distance. Lower down, the Angel has a grey and white stucco, early 19th century, front screening 16th- and 17th-century timberwork over a stone-vaulted 13th-century crypt, while facing Quarry Street is the smiling front to Woolworths, by Thomas Sharp, in white plaster incorporating the sign of the Lion Hotel demolished 1957. Between here and the bridge is new commercial development and an old people's centre in dark brick by P. Shepheard and F. Kennedy-Hawkes (1971–2) bridging a new road near the river.

High Street jumps the river

Wey with an iron bridge and ends with a bang at St Nicholas Church on the junction of the Portsmouth Road. Of the periodically flooded medieval church the 15th-century Losely chapel survives but the rest was rebuilt at a higher level in a heavy neo-13th-century style with apse and central tower, by E. Christian from a plan by Teulon in 1875. Dr Monsell, the hymn writer, was killed by falling stone when surveying progress of his church. It has glass by Clayton and Bell, Victorian Gothic font with lofty, gilded canopy, and an oblique view

down into the Losely Chapel where are monuments to the More and More Molyneux family of Loseley—and a canopied tomb of Arnold Brocas, rector 1387–95.

Back again across the river in Quarry Street, the most picturesque in the town, is Guildford's oldest church, St Mary's, built on the slope above the Wey and steeply stepped inside. The tower is pre-conquest, with pilasters extending to the ground. The chancel and transepts are late 11th century and the body is largely a late 12th-century rebuilding (rare in itself) with apsidal N and S chapels

added in the same century. The chancel, too, had an apsidal end which was cut off in 1825 to widen Quarry Street. Its vault has two tiers of dogtooth mouldings on its ribs and piers of clustered shafts. The N chapel shows fading 13th-century frescoes of St John the Baptist and St John the Evangelist. Alongside No. 6 Quarry Street, which has simple patterns of late 17th-century pargeting (rare in Surrey), is Rosemary Alley, step-

Guildford High Street

Onslow Almshouses, **Guildford**

ping down to the river to give views of the backs of Quarry Street houses, while further along on the E side of the street, are the 18th-century Palladian Castle House and then the Guildford Museum housed in an old cottage extended in neo-Jacobean by Ralph Nevill in 1911, built into the outworks of the Castle. The Museum is the headquarters of the Surrey Archaeological Society, founded 1845. Its collections include finds from Mesolithic dwellings in West Surrey and the Saxon cemetery at Guildown, 13th-century tiles from Chertsey, and exhibitions

illustrating the Wealden forest glass and iron industries, as well as valuable items from the Surrey Iron Railway (*see* Croydon). The Castle can be entered through the adjoining Castle Arch of 1256 past fragments of 12th-century curtain wall. The grim, plain, 12th-century, keep, 25 feet square and 65 feet high is built on top of an older motte with walls 10 to 14 feet thick of chalk and Burgate stone with some Roman bricks. Its roof is a public view-point overlooking the site and the Wey valley, and is reached past the late Norman oratory in the SW corner of the tower and the

only remnant of interest inside. At No. 3 Castle Hill, the home of his unmarried sisters, C. L. Dodgson (Lewis Carroll) died in 1898. He is buried in the cemetery on the Mount and some of his relics are in the Museum and Muniments Room.

S of Castle Hill in Rack's Close, a little park in a disused quarry, are entrances to old clunch mines later used as Castle cellars. High Street can be regained by way of Millbrook along the valley bottom, past the Yvonne Arnaud Theatre (J. E. A. Brownrigg 1969), prettily set on a promontory in the river adjoining the large brick mill-house which has supplied water to Guildford since 1766. The Theatre has a horseshoe plan and a regular pattern of vertical asbestos-cement sun-breakers which looks best through the riverside willows. Across the adjoining mill-pond is Plummers store (consulting architect Brownrigg) which echoes in its riverside curve that of the Theatre.

The W side of the river can be reached by a bridge alongside the theatre. To the S on a sandy promontory, dominating an old ferry point on the "Pilgrim's Way" beyond the wooded houses on the Portsmouth Road, is the ruin of St Catherine's chapel, a roofless early 14th-century rect-angle in sandstone rubble and ashlar dressing, gemlike in pleas-ing decay. Joining the Ports-mouth Road at its High Street bridgehead is the Mount, climb-ing steeply up the chalk spur leading to the Hog's Back. The sites of the Saxon cemetery and of the modern cemetery (with Lewis Carroll's grave) are above the mainly Victorian cottages and from here the full length of the High Street can be seen across the valley. Northwards, across a sea of semis is the clay mound of Stag Hill, on which stand the largest modern buildings of the town, the Cathedral and the University of Surrey. The Cathedral, dedicated to the Holy Spirit, was designed by Edward Maufe who won an open competi-tion in 1932. It is simple, soft, late Gothic, cruciform in plan, with a bulky, unfinished looking, tower but has a noble simplicity in its interior with tall arcades to the naves, tiny clerestory windows and tall narrow aisles each side, all white plastered between Doulting stone dressings. The best views are down the high narrow aisles. The engraved glass of the

Yvonne Arnaud Theatre, **Guildford**

W doors and S Transept is by John Hutton, the St John over the S transept and the Cruci-fixion on the E Wall are by Eric Gill and E window by Moira Forsyth. The University build-ings are set round the N and E sides of the Hill. The main quad and semi-quad, yellow-brick teaching blocks by Building Design Partnership in an industrial building system neatly stepping down the slopes, were begun in 1966. Smaller residen-tial blocks with heavy sloping roofs (the "Diddy houses") by Maguire and Murray (1969) slide down the Hill's E flank. Land-scaping of the site by Derek Love-joy should unify the site and prove the most attractive feature of the Hill.

N-E of Stag Hill is Stoughton, where are the barracks of the W.R.A.C., which was formerly the depot of the Queen's Royal West Surrey Regiment, second oldest in the British Army. Its gigantic, many coloured, brick entrance tower was built in 1876. S towards the town centre, on the edge of Stoke Park and and the town's northern by-pass, is the church of St John the Evangel-ist, Stoke by Guildford; mainly 14th century with a 15th-century

105

Ham House: South front

flint-chequered tower, enlarged 1851. It has an 18th-century black marble font, early 19th-century tablet memorials, and a window by F. J. Shields, friend of Rossetti (1888).

The centre can be regained across Stoke Park to London Road or by the towpath along the Wey, canalised in 1653, to the 18th-century wooden crane alongside Guildford Bridge. Much of the bottom end of the

town has been rebuilt and most of the new buildings here show a refreshing modernity not found in most Surrey towns. The best is the Post Office in North Street, which has projecting bronze glazed "gazebos" to its upper floors, designed by the Department of Environment architects with Roman Halter (1973).

Hale [4] Village on NE skirts of Farnham Park with a few solid

Victorian villas and church of St Mark by B. Ferrey (1844) in a romanesque style with E rose window and round S tower. Unattractive brick terraces near the top with fine views S to Hindhead. Beyond is the only good modern building, a new primary school by the County Architect (1969), and then, on the gravelly, gorsy, hill-top Hampshire boundary is a large Iron Age fort.

Ham* [2] A popular residential area between the Thames and Richmond Park entwined by ancient commons. Twentieth-century developments fill the gaps. The church, of St Andrew, E of the Kingston Road, was built in grey brick by E. Lapidge (1831) and extended by S aisle (1857) and red brick chancel by G. F. Bodley (1901).

Facing the commons are 17th- and 18th-century houses: Gordon House, Langham House and Orford Hall (18th), to the W of the main Kingston road, and Sudbrook Lodge (late 17th) and Ormeley Lodge, beautiful early 18th, to the E. To the N are the late 18th-century Grey Court and the Manor House along Ham Street which leads to Ham House on the river and is as much part of Petersham as Ham.

Near the Kingston Road south of the commons are housing schemes by Eric Lyons, the best-known being Parkleys (1956): flats and shops with flat roofs, tilehanging and yellow brick, while near Langham House is Langham House Close, the first Surrey example of the 1960s' architectural "brutalism" a block of two and three storey flats with heavy exposed concrete floors. On Kingston Road, further S, is the monumental neo-classic building incongruously housing the Hawker Aircraft Works, by H. Worthington and N. Dawbarn (1958).

Ham House, the principal monument of Ham, can be approached on foot from the Richmond Road at Petersham past Victorian lodges, or along the towpath, or by car along Ham Street. It is the most important house of its period in the county. "Close to the Thames, in the centre of all rich and verdant

Ham House: North door

beauty, it is so blocked up and barricaded with walls, vast trees, and gates that you think yourself an hundred miles off and an hundred years back." It has not changed much since Horace Walpole described it thus in 1770.

Externally plain, its interior gives an almost complete record of the flamboyant baroque decoration of the time of James II. The original house was built in 1610 by Sir Thomas Vavasour on an H plan, three storeys high in brick with stone dressings and hipped tiled roof. The N elevation with the main entrance is simplified Vavasour, for Jacobean turrets and a bay over the main entrance have been removed. Major alterations were made in 1673–5 by the Duke and Duchess of Lauderdale, who enclosed the space between the wings on the S side, and then extravagantly decorated the interior. This must be seen even though its glory has faded.

The house is entered on the N directly into the Great Hall, which contains portraits by Kneller, Reynolds and Hoppner. The other main items on the ground floor are as follows: the Duchess's bedchamber containing four sea-pieces by W. Van de Velde Jr; the Marble Dining Room with gilt-leather hangings, 18th-century parquetry floor, and, over the fireplace, a picture of the presentation to Charles II of the first pineapple grown in the country (at Dorney House, near Weybridge); the "Volary", originally a bedroom, used as an aviary after the Duchess had been widowed; the painted ceiling in the White Closet by Antonio Verrio; the chapel in the NE wing with late 17th-century fittings. The upper floor is reached by the Great Staircase (1638), whose walnut balustrades are boldly ornamented pierced panels. The

best rooms upstairs are the North Drawing Room with frieze and ceiling (1637) by Kinsman; the Miniature Room (housing Hilliard's miniature of Queen Elizabeth) with frieze and ceiling painted by Francis Cleyn; the Long Gallery, panelled and plastered in 1639, hung with family and royal portraits; the Blue Drawing Room with plastered ceiling, marbled wainscoting and damask hangings; and the Cabal Room or Queen's Bedchamber (intended for Charles II's queen) with elaborately plastered ceiling and 18th-century tapestries by Bradshaw on themes from Watteau and Pater. The house passed through descendants of the Duchess's first marriage, the Tollemaches, to the National Trust in 1948.

The stretch of the Thames nearby is popular; dinghies sail on flooded gravel pits to the W.

Hambledon [7] Scattered village tumbling over low sand hills between Witley and Hascombe. The church of St Peter, in Burgate stone, NE of its main cluster of tilehung cottages, was rebuilt in 1846, save for the 14th-century N arcade and chancel arch. Eric Parker (1870–1955), the Surrey naturalist and writer, is buried in the churchyard. He lived at Feathercombe, a neo-Georgian house by W. Newton (1910) to the N. The conical wooded hill of Hydon's Ball (593 feet) to the NE is the National Trust's memorial to Octavia Hill. The country round, though agriculturally poor, is a delightful jumble of woods and heath, hill and valley, with views, sometimes to the South Downs over the flatter Weald, sometimes to Blackdown and Hindhead and sometimes to Leith Hill and the North Downs beyond.

Hascombe [7] A ribbon of sandstone and tile-hung houses winding between wooded hills S of Godalming. The church of St Peter, prettily set at the junction of two small valleys, was rebuilt by H. Woodyer in 1864, in a late 13th-century style, but with a central E lancet peeping through a buttress, in local stone with a sharp shingled belfry. The interior should not be missed. The apse is dark, warm and richly decorated, the rafters are cusped and gilded, the wall is stencilled to make a kind of reredos, and there is bright stained glass by Hardman and Powell, who also redecorated, in green, brown, gold and red, the 15th-century rood screen. Few village houses are of interest, but Winkworth Farm to the N has a complete 16th-century half-timbered courtyard buried in creeper. This was the home of Dr Fox, founder of a peculiarly Surrey invention, the Roads Beautifying Association, which in inter-war years brightened new roads in the country with expensive flowering shrubs. Half a mile N, on the steep valley side leading to Thorncombe Street, is his arboretum of rare trees and shrubs bequeathed to the National Trust. Lutyens made additions to Hoe Farm (1890) and built the half-timbered Hascombe (1896). The high wooded Hascombe Hill SE of the village has an Iron Age Fort, largely lost in beech.

Haslemere [7] A small town nicely set between high hills on the borders of Sussex and Hampshire. It has long associations with Wealden ironworks though almost without industry today and has become increasingly popular to live in since Victorian times, when writers from George Eliot to Conan Doyle lived here.

Its musical life, annual festival, and motto "Vita musis gratior" are products of Victorian and Edwardian regard for its quiet beauty. Its parish church, St Bartholomew, NE of the centre towards Grayswood, built as a chapel to Chiddingfold in 1363 was, with the exception of the tower and part of the wall of the N aisle, rebuilt in early English style by J. W. Penfold in 1871. Inside are a Victorian font in rich black and red marble, and a Burne-Jones window (1899) commemorating Tennyson, who lived at Aldworth just over the Sussex border 1869–1892 and worshipped here. Towards Shottermill and the Hampshire border, serving intensive new development, are two other churches, St. Christopher, by Charles Spooner (1902), and St Stephen (1838). The old town centre makes a T round the 17th-century-looking brick Town Hall, built in 1814, and a small triangular green with a prominent cross. Behind the Town Hall up Shepherd's Hill, is a row of mixed 17th- and 18th-century tile-hung and brick cottages raised above the road, while on the Green side of the Town Hall in the wide High Street are the early 18th-century fronts of the White Horse and the Georgian Hotels. Further up is the Educational Museum illustrating particularly the natural history of the area and local crafts, founded 1888. Not far N is Beechside, where the Swiss Dolmetsch family reintroduced many early musical instruments. New Place, by C. F. A. Voysey (1897), roughcast and slate, Red Court (in Scotlands Lane) by E. Newton (1894) and other large 19th-century houses are woven into the woods all round, with one grossly inflated by GRP classrooms to form the Olivetti Training Centre (arch. James Stirling 1973). Good new building is otherwise scarce, thanks to over careful control, but delightful wooded-hilly walks survive in all directions.

Haxted [9] Scattered houses on the Kent border NE of Lingfield. There is an attractive, late 18th century, weatherboarded water-mill and a tilehung millhouse now used as a mill museum. Putten-

Hascombe. Interior and exterior

den Manor on the Lingfield road is an early Tudor house of brick and half timber.

Headley [5] A village on the chalk hills SW of Epsom, in real countryside and remarkably unspoilt for a place so close to London, divided between cottages on the Leatherhead road at Tot Hill and younger housing estate plus church and Cock Inn on the Epsom road. Its chief glory is the expanse of gorse, bracken and open sky encroached on only by birch, which makes up the large common of Headley Heath, now National Trust. The church of St Mary, Victorian, lies alongside the site of the medieval church of which a few scraps remain. In spite of Salvin's design of nave and chancel (1855), and Street's broach tower (1859), it is not very pleasing.

The chief houses are Headley Court to the N, large Jacobean-

Newel post by Lutyens in "Hascombe", **Hascombe**

style by E. P. Warren of about 1910, now the R.A.F. rehabilitation centre, and Headley Grove, to the South, dignified late 18th-century stuccoed. The woods and chalk coombes around are delightful, particularly W, down Lodgebottom Lane, where the valley is known (pointlessly, for it is the epitome of English landscape beauty), as "Little Switzerland".

Hersham [5] Originally "Hersham Green" but now outer London surburbia, small houses and little else. The stone church

of St Peter is by J. L. Pearson (1887). William Lilly (1602–81) the famous Jacobean astrologer lived his last years here and is buried at Walton (qv).

Hindhead [7] Greensand, heather, bilberry and pine on the highest point in SW Surrey. "The most villainous spot that God ever made," said Cobbett in 1822 but since then the spread of Scots pine and domesticated rhododendrons has turned the previous barren hill-top with its single building (the Huts Hotel at the cross roads) into place of retire-

ment and resort. Professor Tyndall (Faraday's successor at the Royal Institution) settled here in 1877 and spread its fame. Gibbet Hill with its immense view to the E and S and the Devil's Punch Bowl, the sandy north-sloping coombe round which climbs the Portsmouth Road, were purchased by the National Trust in 1908 through the efforts of Sir Robert Hunter of Haslemere, one of its founders.

Holmbury St Mary [8] The old villages of Felday and Pitland Street were joined in one parish

Winkworth Farm, **Hascombe**

and given this name when Victorians popularised them and built large houses in the pine woods on the enclosing Greensand hills. G. E. Street built himself Holmdale SW of the village in 1873. His first wife died in 1874; he married again in 1876 and his second wife died within that year. The church of St Mary, one of his last works, is largely her memorial, built at his own expense and completed in 1879. Its composition in a Decorated style with a timber belfry and lean-to aisles and a side chapel above the vestries against a pine clad hill is deliberately picturesque. Stained glass is by Clayton and Bell from Street's designs. The tomb of his second wife is under a canopy on the S wall outside the church. Of the important houses, other than Street's, there are Hopedene, a bulky house by Norman Shaw of the same date (1873), Moxley, by B. Champneys (1888) and Joldwyns, originally by Philip Webb but rebuilt in the modern style of the 1930's by Oliver Hill. Holmbury Hill, SW of the village, has Iron Age hill fort and fine views over the Weald.

Holmwood [8] Scattered development along the London–Bognor road on the edge of a large oak-wood common which is now National Trust property. There are churches at North Holmwood, now almost in Dorking, by R. Hawkins (1875) and South Holmwood by J. B. Watson (1838) and J. Wild (1863). A good section of the Roman Stane Street, showing the original metalling, is preserved by the Surrey Archaeological Society at the foot of Redlands Wood, part of the Greensand range which dominates the villages on the W.

Hook* [5] Inter-war estates stretching S of the Kingston By-pass out to Chessington. St Paul's church, in a red-brick Early English style by Carpenter and Ingelow (1881). Harry Hawker, Australian airman who gave his name to Hawker aircraft, is buried here (1921).

Hooley [6] An inter-war estate on the sloping downland between Chipstead church and the London–Brighton road, now stopped from spreading further by green belt controls.

Horley [9] There is a fragment of the medieval village round the church W of the Brighton road. The rest of the town came after the railway in 1841. The church of St Bartholomew is largely a 19th-century rebuilding by A. W. Blomfield (1881). The best feature is the 14th-century tower with its thin shingled spire and bell-chamber set in the SW side. There are two late 14th-century brasses and an early 14th-century effigy of a knight. To the N of the church is the 15th-century diamond-tilehung, timber-framed, Horsham slate-roofed, Olde Six Bells Inn, which composes nicely with views of the church. The modern town centre is half a mile E near the railway. In Vicarage Lane to the NW is an octagonal brick R.C. church by J. H. Alleyn (1962).

Horne [9] Scattered houses in somewhat dull Weald clay country. The church of St Mary stands almost alone. It was brutally restored in 1880 and muddled in the process so that old fragments appear in odd places. The spiky belfry of 1880 is picturesque, but gone is the earlier complete timber tower, which like that at Burstow swept its skirts from its wide belfry to

the ground, as can be seen from an old water-colour in the church.

Horsell [4] The northern fringes of Woking town; till recently heavily wooded common scattered with varied Victorian and later housing, and nursery gardens like other outskirts of Woking, but now taking the brunt of Woking's crude expansion north-westward. St Mary's church set in a still villagey street, has a 15th-century tower in flint, chalk and local sandstone and 15th-century S aisle and S arcade. The rest is rebuilt or renewed. There is a marble monument to James Fenn (1787), with kneeling figures facing across an untidy pile of books.

East Horsley [5] Another of the string of villages between Leatherhead and Guildford: a two-by-half-mile sprawl of inter-war and post-war housing, thick near the railway line to the N and spreading thinner across the main road into woods on the chalk to the S. Most of the housing has mature trees and, judged as suburbia, is pretty—particularly in the gravelled roads near Pennymead Lake. The village is hardly seen from the main road but travellers along it cannot miss the great neo-Romanesque two-storey lodge in red and black brick which marks the original main entrance to Horsley Towers, the home of Earl Lovelace, son-in-law of Byron (see also Ockham). This house has a plain rectangular centre built by C. Barry (1820), which was "improved" by the Earl in various Gothic styles of his own from 1847 onwards. His earlier work

The Weald from Holmbury Hill ▷
Holmbury St Mary

(*below*) **Headley** Heath

114

was sober, e.g. the Perpendicular tower at the W and the hall (technically interesting for the great trusses bent by Lovelace's steam process), but the later tall round tower at the E and the horseshoe cloisters and chapel at the rear were in violent flint and brick Gothic variations. The present access is from the street by way of a smaller neo-Norman lodge, under another arch and then by a curved tunnel into the cloister and out again through a horseshoe arch to the main entrance by the round tower. A dramatic approach to an extraordinary building. Many other buildings in the village, flint and brick bridges to the S and E of the estate, cottages all over the village and around it and a village school are by this amateur architect and engineer. The church of St Martin is less exciting, for it was heavily restored by H. Woodyer in 1869. The tower is plain Norman with 13th-century detail and a late 18th-century rendered upper storey. Internal proportions were improved by Woodyer, who raised the 13th-century chalk arch to the chancel. Fittings include a number of small brasses and an Elizabethan table tomb with alabaster effigies to the Queen's Groom Porter, Thomas Cornwallis (1626).

Further north on the opposite side of the street is Frenchlands' Hatch, low buildings in a quadrangle by Clifford Culpin, landscaped by Brian Robson, for the Architects' Benevolent Society (1958).

West Horsley [5] A simple, quiet version of East Horsley, mainly a single street running N from the Guildford Road with brick and brick-filled half-timbered cottages, some old and some new. There is a pleasant 18th-century pub, the King

William IV, near the centre and the elaborate neo-classical E entrance lodge to Hatchlands (see East Clandon) by H. S. Goodhart Rendel. The village was earlier known as Horsley Green, and its parish church and large manor house are a mile E on the borders of East Horsley. St Mary's is mainly 13th century with flint W tower and dumpy shingled spire: nicely proportioned inside with late perpendicular S aisle and a N aisle widened in the 1869 restoration. There are 13th-century stained glass medallions in the E and N windows of the chancel and monuments, to a 14th-century priest, to Sir Edward Nicholas (d 1669) in an altar tomb attributed to Grinling Gibbons, to Sir John Nicholas (d 1704) with obelisks and cherubs, and to John Kendal (d 1750) with urn, drapes and a rose-tree by Nicholas Read, a pupil of Roubiliac. West Horsley Place, to the N of the church, incorporates a big medieval building much altered and enlarged in the 16th and 17th centuries, and its main feature is the early 17th-century brick S front of ten bays, its centre capped with pediment and Dutch gable. There are late 17th-century stables. S of the church and stretching to the crest of the Downs are the extensive Sheepleas Woods managed by the County Council as a public open space.

Kenley* [6] known for the hilltop RAF airfield that did much for the defence of London in World War II. There is no village, only thousands of acres of well-treed hillsides and inter-war commuters' houses dependent on the Caterham line to London (opened 1856) for their subsistence. There is an early 19th-century milestone in Godstone

Road, line of the Roman Road to Lewes.

Kew* [2] A Georgian Thames-side village with early Victorian fringes and world-famous Botanic Gardens. Its focus is Kew Green, approached from the N over Kew Bridge by J. Wolfe Barry (1903). The first bridge was in 1789; before then there was a ferry to Kew Palace. The pretty, triangular Green encloses the church. On the W side are several villagey houses which grew up following the settlement of members of the royal family at Kew House in the mid 18th century. Cambridge Cottage, early 19th, is now a Botanical Museum. The Herbarium, the residence of the Duke of Cumberland (King of Hanover 1837), now houses the largest collection of plant specimens in the world.

The church of St Anne is of 1714 with several later additions, a dumpy Georgian-looking building with an octagonal cupola over the E end and a portico and bell turret at the W end added by J. Wyattville in 1836. To the original E end B. Ferrey added in 1851 a mausoleum with a half-dome for the Duke of Cambridge, son of George III, and in 1884 the chancel was enlarged by H. Stock and the mausoleum moved E. Stock also added the pink scaliogla columns to the crossing and gold and white columns in the apse. In its narrow churchyard are buried the artists Gainsborough (d 1788) and Zoffany (d 1810).

At the W end of the Green thick iron gates and ornamental stone piers (by D. Burton 1848) form the main entrance to the Royal Botanic Gardens, formed from the amalgamation of two great royal gardens, those of Richmond Lodge and Kew House. Richmond Lodge was S of the present gardens, near Kew Observatory,

but its grounds stretched N along the river right up to Brentford Ferry. Those of Kew House lay on their E, separated by the bridle road from Richmond (roughly the line of Holly Walk). This road was not closed, nor were the gardens finally combined, until 1802.

The Botanic Gardens have a long history. Those of Kew House, which stood near the present Museum III, were famous in John Evelyn's time for the exotic plants established by Sir Henry Capel. No trace of his work survives, but that done by Princess Augusta, mother of George II, and the Earl of Bute in establishing nine acres of "exotic gardens" in 1759 has survived in part and from these descend the Botanic Gardens of today. Most of the present gardens were, however, royal pleasure gardens and owe their present form to this. George II's Queen Caroline commissioned work in the Richmond Lodge gardens, using C. Bridgeman as gardener and W. Kent as architect, though much of this was swept away by Lancelot Brown, who landscaped the middle sections and excavated the present rhododendron dell in 1773. The grounds of Kew House were improved under the direction of W. Chambers, who built the Pagoda at the southern end, a number of mounds capped by small classical temples and the Orangery (now Museum III), as well as a mosque and many other buildings of which few have survived.

After amalgamation the exotic gardens came under the care of Joseph Banks, who greatly enlarged the scope and use of their collection. He was encouraged by

Horsley Towers, East Horsley

West Horsley Place, 1630 ▷
Kew Palace, 1631

George III, who was interested in the transfer of useful plants from one part of the world to another by way of Kew. There were two gardeners from Kew on the "Bounty". After the death of Banks in 1820 the gardens were neglected until public agitation led to the acquisition, in 1840, of 14 acres for the nation. This area was steadily extended by the addition of gardens and parkland from the royal holdings.

The gardens now cover 300 acres. Their main purposes, the study of horticulture and economic botany, have since been met and one of the world's greatest collections established without destroying their peace and beauty. From the main entrance the old botanic gardens are on the left. To the right between the gardens and the river stands the Dutch House, now known as Kew Palace. This has curved gables and carved moulded brickwork in a style popular with London merchants in 1631. It was acquired by the royal family as an annexe to Kew House which lay to the SE but, after a complete rebuilding by Kent, was pulled down again to make way for a larger house which was never completed and has now vanished. George III retired to the Dutch House when his reason gave way and Queen Charlotte died here in 1818. The interior contains relics of its Georgian occupants. Chambers' Orangery of 1761, to the SE near the site of Kew House, was for many years the largest hothouse in the country.

The pond (1847), the Broad Walk to the Dutch House, the Pagoda Vista leading south, and the Cedar Vista in the southern

Kew Gardens: Palm House and Pagoda

gardens were all laid out by W. A. Nesfield. The Palm House, an early essay in glass and iron, is by R. Turner and D. Burton (1844–1848) and the campanile S of the pond was built as its combined chimney and watertower. King William's Temple by J. Wyattville (1837) is decorated within with iron tablets to commemorate British victories between 1760 and Waterloo. Near Kew Road is the flagstaff of Douglas Fir, 225 feet high, erected 1959. To its S is a lodge designed by E. Nesfield (1866), over-crowded with the fascinating flower paintings of 1872–85 by Marianne North, intrepid traveller. To the W, across the Pagoda Vista, is the second of Burton's great glass houses, the Temperate House, designed 1860. At the Richmond end is the Pagoda, Chambers' essay in fantasy, 165 feet and ten storeys high. The ten roofs were once covered with bright coloured iron plates and decorated with glazed iron dragons. Still brightly painted it forms the focus of vistas in the Gardens and from the Old Deer Park to the S. In the SW corner a bird sanctuary surrounds the Queen's Cottage, an early cottage orné with timber framing and thatched roof, used for royal picnics and dating from Queen Caroline's occupation of Richmond Lodge (about 1770). Modern Kew spreads E of the Gardens. Here facing the Thames is the new four-storeyed square Public Record Office, by W. S. Bryant (1974).

Kingston upon Thames* [2] A minor Saxon royal capital, Kingston is the county town of Surrey, although it is within Greater London, and a big, busy bridgehead shopping centre between the Thames and the hills of Richmond Park and Coombe. Its heart is in the gay Market Place

dominated by the Italianate four-towered Town Hall by C. Henman senr. of 1840, which carries a Francis Bird statue of Queen Anne of 1706. Connected by little alleys is the smaller Apple Market, still mainly for fruit.

All Saints, just to its N, is a large town church nearly 150 feet long extensively restored in 1862 and further altered by Pearson in 1887–8 in clever imitation of older work. The crossing is mixed Norman and 13th century but the nave and chancel arches were raised by Pearson, while the upper part of the tower was rebuilt with a pretty brick top in 1708. The nave is wide, with four late 14th-century bay arcades; the N and S chapels are 15th century. There are brasses of 1437 and 1488, a Flaxman monument to Philip Meadows of 1795, with a dangerously detached cherub on a cloud, and a fine seated figure by Chantrey for the Countess of Liverpool (d 1825). Outside are stones marking the site of the Saxon chapel where stood the coronation stone of Saxon kings from Athelstan (AD 925) to Ethelred the Unready (978), until the chapel collapsed in 1730. The stone now stands grimly railed outside the modern Guildhall (by M. E. Webb 1935) to the S of Market Place. S down Surbiton Road are the Law Courts of 1961, buildings of the Technical College, all dispiriting, and Surrey's County Hall, the oldest part with bold tower and irregular gables by C. H. Howell 1893, extended more and more simply from 1930 onwards.

Not far W High Street breaks out along the Thames opposite the park of Hampton Court Palace where endless movement of boats breaks reflections of Kingston Bridge downstream.

pp122/123 ▷

Inside the Palm House, **Kew**

The river is the best thing in Kingston, but most of the town ignores it. Under river and road here passes the aqueduct, built for Wolsey to bring water from Coombe to Hampton Court.

High Street leads back to the Market Place over the Hog's Mill River by the 12th century Clattern bridge. The stone bridge of three arches over the Thames further NW is by E. Lapidge 1828, widened 1914.

Apart from the pompous commercial blocks of the shopping centre, e.g. Bentalls by M. E. Webb (1935), other items of interest are scattered round the dusty edge of the commercial centre. In London Road are Cleeve's Almshouses of 1688 and the Lovekyn Chapel, a chantry rebuilt 1352 and 1586 to become the chapel of Kingston Grammar School, which, founded in 1638, is housed in buildings of 1929. London Road leads up to Kingston Hill, the local "nob hill" (see Coombe). To the S of London Road, facing the Fairfield are the Museum and the neo-Georgian library by A. Cox 1903 and outside is a 13th-century pillar of King John's Palace which stood near the modern Guildhall. In the museum is a zoopraxiscope, forefather of the cinematograph, invented by the native Eadweard Muybridge (d 1904).

Kingswood [6] Patches of mostly 20th-century suburbia in the folds and high ground south of Banstead and Burgh Heath. The older parts are pleasantly wooded. St Andrew's, a copy of a 14th-century church at Shottesbrooke, Berkshire, with a nice

spire, by B. Ferrey (1852), is at the N end. St Sophia, in the more solid suburb of Lower Kingswood to the S, was built in 1891 by Sidney Barnsley for the Byzantine scholar Dr Freshfield, in brick with stone embellishment in free Byzantine style. Inside, the E end is marble lined, while around the squat nave are nine capitals from 4th- to 6th-century Byzantine buildings brought here by Freshfield. The timber pulpit, priests' seats and stalls are by Barnsley, who also painted the pretty wagon roof himself.

◁ Detail of the Geddes window, **Laleham**

Laleham** [2] Small houses and bungalows line the river Thames almost continuously from Laleham upstream to Staines, but to the S of the village is a good open stretch of river and to the E is rich flat farmland, saved from building by Green Belt restrictions. The old village is back from the river on the road from Staines to Shepperton where the church of All Saints punctuates a bend with a squat Georgian brick tower of 1732. Apart from the tower and the Tudor-brick N chapel the exterior looks all 19th century, owing to drastic restoration, but inside it retains medieval interest,

first in its curiously skew plan and then in the two late 12th-century arcades. There are two minor monuments by Chantrey. The stained glass in the W window is a powerful design by the Irish artist Wilhelmina Geddes, showing a ragged St Christopher carrying a somewhat mongoloid infant Jesus. It was designed for the E window in 1926 but moved following protest from some outraged parishioners.

Dr Thomas Arnold taught at Laleham from 1819 to 1828 before moving to Rugby and his son Matthew was born here (1822) and is buried in the churchyard.

Georgian and neo-Georgian at **Laleham**

The built-up area between the church and the river is unattractive in detail, though softened by mature trees, but on the pleasant Green which stretches southwards down to the river are 18th and early 19th century houses, such as Coverts and Muncaster House of the early 18th and Thatched Cottage (suitable *ornée*) of the early 19th. At the S end is Laleham House built for the 2nd Earl of Lucan by J. B. Papworth in 1803.

Leatherhead [5] An historically interesting town, aesthetically ruined since World War II, i.e. under planning control, with a centre which is the meanest of any Surrey town outside Woking. But it lies in attractive scenery and is a good centre for exploring the North Downs before motorways make Leatherhead the Clapham Junction of the motor age. The parish church of Saints Mary and Nicholas, S of the crossroads is the best building in the town. It has a 15th-century flint-faced W tower, well seen from the Mole valley, set slightly skew so that it breaks into the S arcade. The interior has four-bay arcades and carved chalk chancel arch dating from the end of the 12th century but harshly restored. The chancel and transepts were rebuilt in the early 14th. The novelist "Anthony Hope" Hawkins, son of a headmaster of St John's School, is buried in the churchyard (1933). West is the Mansion (c 1739) incorporating parts of the home of the second Lord Howard of Effingham (d 1642). Across the river Mole, here diverted by L. Brown, is Thorncroft Manor House, small plain brick, by Sir Robert Taylor (1770). Between the church and the crossroads is the Thorndike Theatre, by Roderick Ham (1969), neatly built into the shell

of Lovett Gill's cinema of 1954. From hideous buildings at the cross-roads Bridge Street descends W past the early 16th-century Running Horse Inn (made famous by the Elizabethan poet, John Skelton, in the poem "Tunnyng of Elynour Rumming", who "brewed moppy ale" here) to the bridge of fourteen brick arches by G. Gwilt (1782) over the Mole. N of the centre cross-roads are a few old brick and flint cottages, which include the 18th-century timber-framed, Sweech House, restored in 1949–1950 by the local history society. A little N are neo-Georgian Council Offices by Rose and Gardner (1935) on the site of Kingston House where John Wesley preached his last sermon in 1781, and in Kingston Road is All Saints Church by A. Blomfield (1889).

Leigh (pronounced 'lie') [8] A tidy village in a tidy park-like piece of the Weald with views of the North Downs through tall oaks and elms, with a tidy green in the centre fringed by the Plough Inn to the N, church to the NE and cottages and Victorian school on the W. St Bartholomew's is a small, simple, largely 15th century, building in Reigate stone, complicated in 1855 (by H. Woodyer), and extended in 1890 (by F. C. Lees), when the porch was added and the interest of the interior was diminished. Inside are a 15th-century font, an E window by Kempe (1890), and memorial brasses to members of the Arderne family. John Arderne (d 1449) and his wife Elizabeth have full-face figures three-feet high in civilian dress. The Ardernes lived a little N at the moated house, Leigh Place, which retains some 17th-century details but was Gothicised in 1810. The Plough

is 18th-century weatherboarded, overdecorated with 20th-century additions and coloured lights. S of the church is Priest's House, a long half-timbered range with 20th-century extension in old materials. Half a mile SE is the much-altered 17th-century Swain's Farm where Ben Jonson, the Elizabethan dramatist, often retired and 1½ miles SW is Shelwood Manor a rambling house of 17th and later centuries, connected with early Wealden ironmasters.

Limpsfield [6] A varied and attractive parish stretching from Woldingham on the chalk downs to Edenbridge, Kent. The old village consists of one long High Street rising gently southwards and giving views to the high scarp of the Downs. The church of St Peter stands above the street near its N end, approached through a restored 14th-century lychgate. It is picturesque in spite of Pearson's restoration of 1872 with its Horsham-slated roof sweeping down to low side walls and its pyramid-roofed square tower. Most is late 13th century though the tower and west wall are late 12th. Lancet windows in the chancel and chapel are filled with Clayton and Bell glass. Frederick Delius (1862–1934) was buried in the churchyard, as were Florence Barclay (d 1921), author of a best seller *The Rosary*, and the biologist Sir J. Arthur Thomson (1935). The High Street is full of attractive buildings from the 15th to the 19th centuries. The most picturesque groups are Detillens Cottages, and the Forge Cottages and Chapel Cottages on W side. In the Manor House near the church lived Eugenia Stanhope, who married Lord Chesterfield's son and published the *Letters to His Son*. Up the A25 and beyond

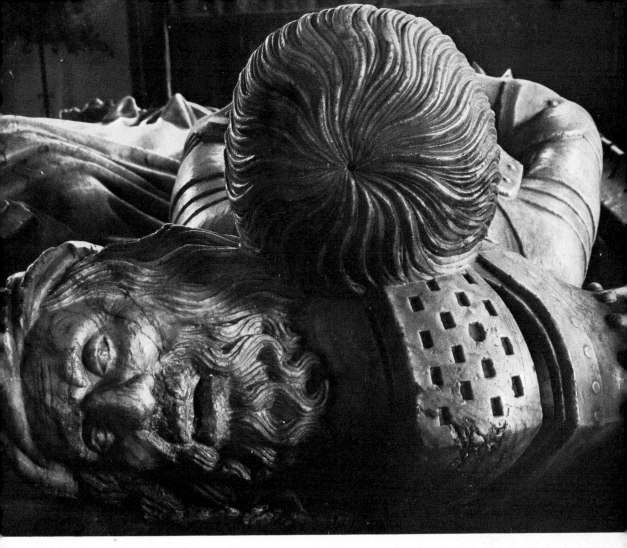

(*opposite*) The First Lord Cobham and (*above*) Sir Reginald Cobham in **Lingfield** Church

Limpsfield Common is *Limps-field Chart*, a 19th-century suburb with St Andrew's Church, by A. Blomfield (1895). The road E leads into thick mixed woodland with occasional dramatic views of the Greensand hills in Kent and the Weald. In the Weald S of the village are the 15th-century Stockendon and Grants Farm-house, typical of many in the area.

Lingfield [9] A large village com-paratively isolated, as Surrey villages go, in the SE corner of the county. Historically interest-ing and in parts picturesque though post-war shops in the centre give a bad impression. The old village developed within a quadrilateral of surrounding roads and the best of it is in small parcels, round the pond at the SW corner and the church at the NE. It became important when the third Lord Cobham of Ster-borough founded a college for secular priests and rebuilt the church, joining it to the college buildings, in 1431. The church is now the only large perpendicular church outside St John's Croydon, with nave of four generous bays and N and S aisles. The chancel has N and S chapels but the S aisle and the S chapel are shorter than those on the N, so that the interior has a lopsided look and appears to have two naves and chancels, the more so because the principal monument in the true chancel obscures the view of the altar. The late medieval fittings and monuments justify a special journey. There are 15th-century timber screens between the chancel and the chapels. The stalls on the W and S are also 15th-century and have a fine set of misericords. The bench with royal arms and medallion heads on the N side is 16th century and must have been brought from elsewhere as the choir stalls have been cut to fit it in. The best tombs are of the Cobham family. The first Lord Cobham in the N chapel (d 1361) has a tomb chest surmounted by an armoured recumbent effigy with his feet resting on a melancholy Saracen. In the centre of the chancel is that to Sir Reginald Cobham (d 1446), the founder of the college, and his wife with alabaster effigies, and in the N chapel is a third altar tomb, to Sir Thomas Cobham (1471).

The church also contains the best set of brasses in Surrey. In the chancel are four priests, of 1445, 1458, 1469 and 1603, and a girl with no inscription. In the N chapel on his altar tomb is a brass of Regl. second Lord Cobham (1403) and also life-size figures of Eleanor wife of Sir Regl. Cobham (d 1420), another to a lady, perhaps Elizabeth, first wife of second Baron, with a pet dog, and to Katherine Stokett (d 1420).

The College was dissolved in 1544 though a late 17th-century farmhouse, of brick, tilehanging and Horsham slates, stands on its site, and the college Guest House, N of the church, survives as a county library. The best view in Lingfield is at the SE entry to the churchyard where a range of late 17th-century brick buildings faces a group of 15th and 16th-century timber framed. At the S end the 16th-century wing has a rare contemporary shop front (now unhappily filled in), which was used as a butcher's shop till the 1950s.

SW of the church in Plaistow Street, overhung with trees and adjoining the pond, is the prominent Cage, a stone cage of 1773 added to a stepped 15th-century cross. SE of Lingfield is the popular racecourse, opened 1890. Of Sterborough, the mid-14th-century castle of the Cobhams on the Kent boundary two miles E, only the moat and traces of the plan (four towers and a gate, like Bodiam) remain.

Littleton ** [2] A tadpole of a parish, squeezed between Laleham and Shepperton, with its head almost wholly submerged in the huge Queen Mary reservoir. The historic centre, near the waist, consists of the church, Manor House and Manor Farm and is almost unnoticed between the bank of the great reservoir and the Shepperton Studios of British Lion Films. The old village, in spite of its bulky neighbours, still retains a rural air, for the little river Ash sharply divides it from the spread of Shepperton Green to the SW. The church of St Mary Magdalene was founded in the 12th century by monks from Chertsey Abbey, but most of the present building, in chalk rubble, flint and brick with Reigate Stone dressings, is of the 13th. The nave was heightened and the W tower added in brick in the 16th century. The tower was given its high parapet in the 18th and the N chapel (now vestries) was added in 1705 as a mortuary chapel for the Wood family. Inside, the nave is short and the chancel dark and low but the fittings include medieval pews, early 18th-century pulpit, early 16th-century chancel screen, richly carved choir stalls and wall panelling of the 15th century brought here from Winchester Cathedral, late 17th-century Flemish communion rails with high relief panels. In the chancel

is a window, based on a John Millais painting, given by his widow in memory of his many happy visits to the village. The rectory to the SE is a brick building dated 1699 while the Manor House and Manor Farm form a group of picturesque but much altered 16th- and 17th-century buildings.

The Queen Mary Reservoir is one of the largest in the world and holds enough water to supply London for a month. It was completed in 1925 and incorporates a wide breakwater ¾ mile long.

British Lion Studios buildings are of gaunt ugliness, the worst being the most recent three-storey open-ended garage block north of the church, a sad commentary on planning control.

Littleton [4] A hamlet of hearty timber-framed cottages with some prefabricated timber bungalows, serving the Loseley estate. The little church of St Francis (1843) is inset in the former village school.

Long Ditton * [2] Now one of the western extensions of 19th- and 20th-century Surbiton. The gentle leafy character is going fast as more and more houses are squeezed into older larger gardens. St Mary's church by G. E. Street, completed 1880, replaces one by Sir Robert Taylor. Inside are stone fragments and a brass of 1527 saved from the medieval church. George Evelyn (1530–1603), grandfather of the diarist, manufactured gunpowder here and at Wotton and Godstone.

Loseley [4] W of Littleton and S of the sandy ridge which carries the "Pilgrim's Way" is Loseley House, the best Elizabethan house surviving in Surrey. It was built in

Loseley

1562 for Sir William More, one of the Queen's counsellors, and is still occupied by his descendants. A wing added by Sir George More (d 1632) was pulled down in the 19th century. Sir George's daughter ran away from here to her secret marriage with John Donne. The main range is in Burgate stone, with whitened clunch dressings from Waverley Abbey (qv), and has attractive, asymmetrical elevations. The handsome baroque entrance door on the N was inset about 1680, though it originally led into the Great Hall and not into the present entrance hall. The Great Hall contains portraits of Edward VI, Elizabeth I (by Zucchero), James I (by Mytens) and a group of Sir More Molyneux and his family by Somers (1739), which is handsomely set above the carved Tudor panelling brought here from Nonsuch (*see* Ewell) in the late 17th century. Next door is the library in a 19th-century Jacobean style but containing an overmantel of 1570; then the dining-room which has a delicate late 16th-century ceiling with frieze of cockatoos and moorhens and a massive two-tiered fireplace carved in solid clunch. Upstairs, James I's bedroom has a Belgian tapestry of 1650 and Queen's Elizabeth's bedroom a 17th-century tapestry from Mortlake. The house is often open to the public during the summer. The important N front can be seen from the footpath between Littleton and Compton.

Lowfield Heath [9] A piece of early ribbon development on the Brighton Road just N of Crawley, it has been beheaded and may be

Lowfield Heath: The west window

removed by Gatwick Airport. St Michael's church is a charming work by Wm Burges (1867).

Its best features are the thick rose-window on the W and the *art nouveau* stained glass in the E windows.

Lyne [1] 19th- and 20th-century cottages with scattered mansions west of Chertsey. Holy Trinity Church is by F. Francis (1849), a

vigorous cruciform pointed church set in mature trees. The Alm'ners, or Almner's Priory, on the Chertsey road, has 15th-century remnants of the house of the Almoner of Chertsey Abbey, part of its ancient garden and fishpond.

Malden* [2] At Old Malden on a tiny wooded bluff above the open valley of the Hog's Mill River are

the church and 18th-century Manor House and Manor Farm. The rest of Malden as far as the foot of Coombe Hill is London suburbia. The original chancel of St John's church had medieval flint walls and there was a brick nave and plain W tower of 1610. When a new nave and chancel by T. G. Jackson were added in 1875, the old became a S aisle and chapel. The Victorian Caen stone

132

pulpit has high relief alabaster panels. Lord Chancellor Walter de Merton founded his family college here in 1263 but moved it to Oxford the following year. New Malden station is distinguished by two seventeen-storey office blocks in white concrete panels.

Merrow [5] Between Merrow Down, celebrated in Kipling's *Just-So Stories*, and E suburbs of Guildford. The parish church of St John was rebuilt by R. C. Hussey in 1842, but a few medieval fragments were incorporated, including the 12th-century N doorway and arches of the S arcade. Members of the Onslow family of Clandon Park are buried in the churchyard. Across the narrow flint-walled Trodds Lane which carries never-ending A25 traffic, is a three-storeyed roughcast pub dated 1615.

Merstham [6] An old quarry village and a modern housing estate at the foot of the North Downs escarpment, divided by the Brighton road and railway. The old village, to the W, worked hearthstone reserved for Westminster Abbey and other royal buildings, for it was one of the few building stones in the SE. St Katharine's church is on a knoll ringed with trees to the N isolated by the construction of the M25 motorway between it and late 18th-century Palladian stuccoed rectory. St Katharine's is mainly 13th-century, with a large 13th-century tower capped with 14th-century shingled spire. The W doorway is 13th-century with trefoiled arch and contemporary door. The interior is plastered throughout. It has big square late 12th-century Sussex marble font, a number of brasses, the best being the figures of two wives on the table tomb of John Elingbridge (d 1473) and a tablet in relief to George Jolliffe, killed 1797 at the Battle of the Nile.

Part of the first public railway, **Merstham**

S of the Rectory leading to the Brighton road is Quality Street (a name that appealed to James Barrie), with mixed 16th- to 19th-century houses in pleasant harmony. New Merstham E of the railway is the worst designed estate of the former London County Council; built in 1948, in what should have been London's Green Belt. The Surrey Iron Railway, the first public railway in the world, reached here in 1805. Its overgrown cutting can be seen along the Brighton road at the top of the hill and a sample of the line, flanged rails on stone sleepers, just S of the Jolliffe Arms.

Merton * [3] Important in the Middle Ages for its Augustinian Priory and later for its factories based on the water power of the river Wandle. The Priory was founded in 1116 and became one of the wealthiest in England. Archbishop Thomas à Becket and Walter de Merton were both educated here. It was dissolved in

haste in 1538 and its stone carried off to build the palace at Nonsuch (*see* Ewell). Only fragments of the priory exist today. The site of its high altar is marked by an inscribed stone just N of Station Road hedged by crude industrial buildings. The chancel and nave lay diagonally across Station Road with the cloister and chapter house on the track of the railway. Parts of the priory wall can be seen in Station Road to the W— and E of the Pickle (corruption of Pike Hole, a branch of the Wandle) within the metal works. A Norman doorway of about 1175 found at Abbey House was re-erected in the wall of the parish churchyard. The chapter house was often used for meetings of Parliament and in 1235 the Statute of Merton was passed here, by which the earls and barons declined to introduce certain rules of canon law into English law.

St Mary's, the parish church, is a mile W beyond Merton Park

133

Station in an area developed by John Innes in the 19th century. Here was the John Innes Horticultural Institute until its move to Hertfordshire in 1950. The estate is much as Innes left it; tilehung and half-timbered houses in gardens bounded by holly facing avenues of chestnut trees. The Norman nave of the church has a N doorway with a zig-zag decoration. The chancel is early 13th century with tall blank arcading and an early 15th-century hammerbeam roof. It contains monuments to Sir Gregory Lovell (d 1597), treasurer of Queen Elizabeth's household, and his two wives, with alabaster kneeling figures, and to the Smith family by R. J. Wyatt (1832) for the widow of Captain Cook, who lived here. The memorial window to John Innes in the S aisle is by Burne-Jones (1907) and was executed at the Morris Works at Merton Abbey. At the W end are hatchments of Sir William Hamilton and Lord Nelson, who worshipped here after they had set up joint house at Merton Place in 1801. This was Nelson's last home in England. It stood E of the present South Wimbledon Station, was sold to pay Lady Hamilton's debts, and demolished in 1840.

Silk weaving was established on the Wandle in the 17th century. William Morris moved his workshops from London to old weaving sheds on the northern part of the priory site in 1881. These closed in 1940 but Arthur Liberty of Regent Street had acquired the silk printing works a little further S, which still continue. They enclose one of the old Wandle undershot waterwheels, together with an old colour-house of flint and brick dated 1742. High Street runs N of the priory site and has the river running alongside for a short distance. It is difficult to see in it today the village street of Merton,

overshadowed by the vast Board Mills and Apex Tower (1966), a dark grey seventeen-storey block of offices E of Colliers Wood Station, but further W in Kingston Road and nearer the church, fragments of the village character remain e.g. in the Manor House, 17th and 18th century with timber frame, and late 18th-century brown brick Dorset Hall.

Mickleham [5] In the Mole's gorge through the North Downs, along the old highroad to Dorking, in some of the loveliest scenery in Surrey. The church of St Michael is of Norman foundation, but has been much altered. The Norbury chapel on the N side is early 16th-century and is walled in chequered flint and clunch, a rare example in Surrey. The church was drastically restored in 1891 by Ewan Christian who gave it a new E end and added a chubby round tower on the S side. The E end has 16th-century Flemish stained glass. In the Norbury chapel is the table tomb of William Wyddowson (d 1518) and his wife with canopy cut into the wall. Within its arch are lively figured brasses. Fanny Burney and George Meredith were both married in the church. Fanny Burney was an associate of the group of intellectual French refugees centred on Juniper Hall, near the foot of Box Hill, married General d'Arblay, and settled at Fetcham and then Westhumble. Opposite the church is the attractive 17th-century Running Horses Inn and to N is Old House with elaborate brickwork dated 1636 altered in the 18th century. To the S facing Juniper Hall and Box Hill across the Lodgebottom Valley is Juniper Hill, by J. Staff (1780) with an Ionic porch and a central pediment.

Milford [7] A few brick and tile cottages around cross-roads at the

end of the Guildford–Godalming By-pass, blown out with late 19th- and 20th-century houses into a place with no sensible plan or centre.

The church of St John is of 1844, and 1859, Milford House, on the Godalming Road, is a vigorous three-storey brick house of 1730 with stone dressing. Near the station is Rake Manor built in 1602 but restored and extended first by R. Nevill, then by Lutyens, and then by Baillie Scott. Amberley Farm, on Elstead Road, and Mousehill are late 17th-century brick, stone and tilehung, gabled buildings.

Mitcham* [3] A vigorous Cockney suburb with the air of a country town, famous for its fair, cricket and lavender. The lavender fields have gone but the fair comes annually and cricket is played on the Cricket Green surrounded by traces of medieval and 18th-century Mitcham.

The parish church of Saints Peter and Paul, W of the Green, is a simplified Perpendicular style church of 1821 by G. Smith with a medieval NW tower. The interior, restored by S. Dykes Bower in 1951, has a high, nicely vaulted roof and contains a large monument with medallion portraits to Sir Ambrose Crowley (d 1713) and Lady Crowley (1727), tablets by R. Westmacott and H. Weeks and a wall monument with portrait relief by P. Rouw.

Cricket Green is the centre and most attractive part of Mitcham. On its W is an ugly town hall of 1887 but around are the pretty 1812 schools, early 19th-century stuccoed Elm Lodge and White House on the NE, the Methodist church by E. Mills (1958), late 17th century, colour-washed brick, Canons near the SE corner, the single-storey almshouses of 1829, and early 18th-century

three-storey, stock brick, King's Head Hotel at the corner of London Road.

S down London Road is Mitcham Station, a two-storey, stock brick building with a central arch. Here the Surrey Iron Railway, the first public railway in the world, crossed the road on its way from Wandsworth to Croydon in 1803 and though the railway is a few years older than the house, the latter may be the oldest railway station in the world.

Further S in Riverside Drive is Wandle House in brick and Portland stone of about 1790 resembling the Wick, Richmond, and probably by Robert Mylne. N is Upper or Fair Green, which was the site of the historic fair till 1923. It is now a shambling road junction with poles and signs instead of trees. N of this is Eagle House, two-storeyed, of stock brick with red brick dressings and a tall slate roof, built 1705.

Further N are a few more old houses grouped near the Swan Inn and beyond near the Tooting border is St Barnabas, a large church by H. P. Burke-Downing (1914), while to the W in Phipps Bridge Road are more 18th- and 19th-century houses. One is a round tower of rubble from old London Bridge. To the E is Mitcham Common whose ancient flat dull character has now been enlivened (and may yet be improved) by many years of refuse dumping. The fair is held here each August.

East Molesey [2] An overgrown village at the confluence of the Mole with the Thames, opposite Hampton Court Palace. Older parts lie back while newer development nearer the river suffered

Merstham

badly from floods which its existence has exacerbated. The newest of all is sadly on the once-famous Hurst Park race-course. The river Mole took its name from Molesey (not vice versa) and is known locally as the Ember. St Mary's parish church, was rebuilt by T. Bury in 1865, while Kemp Town, W of the old village which was laid out fairly generously in mid 19th century has its own church, St Paul, by Salter and Laforest, in 1856. The Bell just S of St Mary's is a 16th-century timber-framed, rendered pub. Few other buildings of note, survive, but the Jacobean-style brick railway station, 1849, called "Hampton Court" (not Molesey) is one.

West Molesey [2] Dull sister of East Molesey; much is 20th-century light industry, in sheds screened by pompous office blocks on wide streets used as car parks. The parish church has a 15th-century W tower of ragstone but was otherwise rebuilt in light-yellow brick in 1843. The pulpit, complete with back and sounding board, is Jacobean.

Morden* [3] A gigantic London suburb centred on the terminus of the world's longest tunnel, that of the Northern Line, which reached here in 1928.

It was a tiny village till the 20th century and the population of the parish was only 980 in 1901.

The church of St Lawrence and Morden Park, house and grounds, lie a mile S of the present centre. The other great house of the village, Morden Hall in its park, is to the E. Both have been acquired by the National Trust, together with other open spaces along the Wandle. St Lawrence was completely rebuilt in 1636, a rare period for English churches, in red brick with stone quoins. The windows are in a Perpendicular style,

Newdigate

said to have come from the older church but more likely just another Surrey anachronism. Inside is an unspoilt village church. The pulpit with sounding board, the three-sided communion rail and the W gallery are of 1720. There are a number of wall monuments to the Garths of Morden Hall, a large monument with a fine bust to Sir Peter Leheup (1777) and

17th-century glass in the E window with figures of Moses and Aaron. To the W of the church is the 18th-century landscape of Morden Park with a large, stock brick house of 1770 with a contemporary interior. In Central Road, a little E, is the Old School House of 1731 and just S are the Earl Haig Homes by Grey Wornum and L. de Soissons (1931 on).

Morden Hall is a dull 18th-century building made duller by mid-19th-century cement rendering, but it retains the original staircase with Palladian balustrades. It was the home of the Garth family, then of Abraham Goldsmid, who bought Merton Place to help Lady Hamilton, and later of the Hatfeilds, snuff merchants, who presented the house and park to the National Trust. The Park has 18th-century garden ornaments and, on the Wandle, two 18th-century snuff mills with undershot waterwheels.

The prominent curved slab of offices W of the Underground station is Crown House by A. Green (1961).

In the huge St Helier Estate to the SE, designed by G. T. Forrest, chief architect to the London County Council in the 1930s, are an unfinished church, St Peter's, by C. Nicholson (1932) and Bishop Andrews's church by G. Hyslop (1933).

Mortlake* [2] A Thames-side village best known as the finish of the Oxford-Cambridge boat-race near its prominent brewery. Little of the river can be seen from the High Street and its great bend has to be found down alleyways.

The church of St Mary was founded in 1348 but almost entirely rebuilt by A. Blomfield, the chancel in 1885 and the nave and S aisle in 1905. The Perpendicular W tower (1543) and late 17th-century vestry survive from the earlier church, as do the octagonal Perpendicular font presented by Archbishop Bourchier and monuments to Francis Coventry (1699), Nicholas Godschall (1748), both with good figures, and Viscountess Sidmouth (1811) by R. Westmacott. Sidmouth himself, born Henry Addington, Prime Minister 1801-1804 (d 1844), is buried in the churchyard. Between the church and Thames were the Mortlake Tapestry works, founded in 1619. There is a panel of its 17th-century tapestry behind the vicar's stall in the church.

There are distinguished houses still in the High Street E of the church. No. 123, which has an early 18th-century interior and a later Georgian front with Tuscan portico, had the distinction of being painted twice by J. M. W. Turner, and there is a group of 18th-century houses on the river between the Brewery and Chiswick Bridge (by Herbert Baker, 1937).

S of the church is a Roman Catholic burial ground containing the huge stone tent, decorated with crescents and stars, over the grave of Sir Richard Burton (d 1890), explorer of Arabia and the Nile and translator of the Arabian Nights.

For Munstead *see* Busbridge.

Newchapel [9] A cross-roads on the London-Eastbourne road W of Lingfield with a large fake-Elizabethan manor built (1908) for the Pears soap magnate and the Mormons' "London Temple," a simple, white, rectangular block with a narrow tower and spire, by U.S. architect Edward Anderson (1958). It is made up of a series of rooms with no church hall, contrary to its appearance, and is not open to the public.

Newdigate [8] A wide-spreading Wealden village with no real centre. Its traditional place of assembly is the Brocas field, N of St Peter's church. The church, much restored and altered, has an impressive 14th-century timber tower carried on four oak posts 17 inches square. The base is weatherboarded, the next stage is sloping shingles, the next a weatherboarded belfry and the highest a shingled spire. The construction of its posts and diagonal bracing can be seen in the gloomy interior. The chancel has late 13th-century lancets and most of the nave is 14th-century; the N arcade was rebuilt with piers and arches copying the 14th-century S arcade, when the N aisle was built in 1877. In this aisle medieval glass panels show ogee canopies and three bears' paws, arms of the Newdigate family. Home Farm, half mile, is one wing of the earlier Newdigate Place which was a timber-framed quadrangle of the 16th century. The area is scattered with half-timbered buildings, but most have been much restored and altered.

To the N, Ewood was important for its medieval iron forges worked from a large lake now lost in woodland.

New Haw [5] Untidy development south of Addlestone near the junction of Basingstoke Canal with Wey Navigation, dull Ministry of Works buildings for the Veterinary Research Labs (1956) to the W and a huge "super-grid" switching station on Wey meadows to the E.

Norbury* [3] Between the northern end of Croydon and the southern end of London, but distinguished from both by substantial Edwardian housing. St Stephen in Warwick Road is a red and yellow brick Perpendicular style church by W. S. Weatherley (1908).

Normandy [4] William Cobbett 1726-1835) was born at Farnham, eight miles W and made his last home here at Normandy Farm now called Cobbett Hill) on gently rolling heavy lands N of the Hog's Back. The village straggles along the Aldershot-Guildford

Boswell's Farm (see **Oakwood**)

road with no real centre or good group of buildings. S of the railway is a separate rectangle of bungalows and wire, called Christmas Pie. N of the main road are wide heathlands saved from building by the Army's use as training grounds, and in these is Henley Park, the estate given by Queen Elizabeth I to the Earl of Essex. The present much-altered house dates from 1751. At Wyke, on the road to Aldershot is St Mark's, Woodyer's first church (1847).

Norwood* [3] A suburban, well-treed, ridge N of Croydon, de-corated with a B.B.C. television mast at the N end and the I.T.V. mast on Beulah Hill at the S. Beulah Hill had a short-lived spa in the 19th century and Upper Norwood still retains the happy atmosphere of early Victorian expansion in its wide roads and Italianate villas. The prominent church with W tower and spire is All Saints, by James Savage (1829). Architecturally more important is St John the Evangelist in Sylvan Road, one of the best churches by J. L. Pearson (1887), in an Early English style, twin-turreted and red brick outside and stock brick and stone ribs inside.

It has a stone screen and stained-glass windows by N. Comper, who worshipped here. At Selhurst Road in South Norwood is Holy Innocents, a good large stone church by Bodley (1885). Nearby is South Norwood Lake, once the reservoir of the vanished Croydon Canal.

Nutfield [6] A harsh-looking village of dark cottages along the sandstone ridge carrying the Redhill–Godstone road A25. The parish church of Saints Peter and Paul on the N side commands the wide belt of Holmsdale that separates the ridge from the North

138

Downs. It is largely 13th century, much altered by W. O. Milne in 1882. The tower is Perpendicular with brick top of 1786. The rood screen is 16th century and the octagonal font 15th century on a stem of 1665. The E and the SE windows are by Burne-Jones of 1890 and 1891. In the chancel is a brass of Wm Graffton (d 1465) described as a priest but wearing lay clothes and shown with his wife. Nutfield Priory to the SW is the largest Victorian house in grim Tudor style by J. Norton (1871). On both sides of the ridge are extensive excavations for fuller's earth, a rare clay used for purifying oils and exported all over the world. Nutfield Marsh, a separate hamlet to the N has a number of old cottages.

South Nutfield [6] South Nutfield is late 19th- and 20th-century development near the station on the Redhill–Tonbridge line. There is a chemical factory. It has a hot-red brick church of 1888.

Oakwood [8] Wealden meadow and coppice woodlands with no real village and the most isolated church in Surrey, hidden in a clearing of dense woodland, now more ash than oak. St John the Baptist was built with nave and chancel as one about 1220 but was doubled by Basil Champneys, who added the large N aisle (1879). The sweeping Horsham slate roof and graveyard surrounded by woods are more attractive than the interior. The E windows have triangular heads (cf. Chipstead); there is a brass of 1431 and a black marble Victorian font.

The nearest settlements are the hamlet of Oakwoodhill to the S with a nice 17th-century pub, and the mixed village of Walliswood to the W.

Just over the parish boundary of Ockley is Boswells Farm, a rare,

Ockham

unrestored 16th-century, cruciform, timber-framed house used as kennels by the Surrey Union Hunt.

Ockham [5] A quiet village S of the London–Guildford road, with mid-19th-century, decorated-brick estate cottages set back from the road in well-kept gardens. The estate belonged to the Lovelace family, who altered Horsley Towers; village improvements became their hobby. The church of All Saints is almost hidden in the big trees of Ockham Park. Its best-known feature is the rare 13th-century E window of seven lancets, tallest at the centre, grading down each side. Within, the lights are divided by Sussex marble shafts capped with stiff foliage. It is set in a four-centred arch and the outer capitals appear to have been altered to fit, as though the whole window had been brought from elsewhere, such as Newark Priory. The body of the church appears 13th-century although the tower with its big blocks of chalk is largely 15th-century and a simple brick chapel was added (1735) as a mausoleum for the King family. This contains a magnificent monument with fine figures to

Peter, first Lord King, Lord Chancellor of England, who died in 1734, and his wife, by Rysbrack and also a bust by R. Westmacott to the seventh Lord King (d 1833) and a stone casket to the second Earl of Lovelace (d 1906). The chancel windows contain some 15th-century figures on the S and glass in the E window by T. G. Jackson. The S side of the nave has some early 18th-century Flemish glass. The brass to Walter Frielende (1376), N of the altar, is the earliest brass of a priest in the county. The house of Ockham Park was built by Hawksmoor in 1725 but destroyed by fire in 1948, leaving only an orangery and stables, since altered. This was the home of the Kings. One married Byron's daughter and became first Earl of Lovelace. William of Occam, the medieval philosopher, 1280–1349, was probably a native.

Ockley [8] Stretching along the Roman road to Chichester and round a long green of varying width with buildings of all dates. On the W side the most determinedly picturesque cottages, employing timber frames, brick, stone and tile hanging, are of the 19th-century. Leith Hill and the high sandstone escarpment form a backcloth to the green but views are delicate and could be ruined by widening of the narrow road which is still the main route from London to western Sussex. The parish church of St Margaret is three-quarters of a mile NE, alone save for Ockley Court (a spoilt 18th-century brick house) and the site of a 12th-century castle. The church contains work of the 14th century, a 15th-century timber porch and a Perpendicular W tower rebuilt in 1700, but most was rebuilt in 1873 when the chancel was lengthened and a N aisle added. The present fittings nearly

all date from the rebuilding. Jayes Park, the elegant stock brick house NW of the village, incorporates fragments of 17th-century building, but the main elevation toward Ockley was rebuilt in 1913.

Ottershaw [4] Halfway between the Thames meadows and Woking heaths, mostly small 19th- and 20th-century houses with some large 19th-century estates. Christchurch is a grim building by Gilbert Scott (1864) in many-coloured bricks and stone with a tower and broach spire added in 1885. Whitewashed and dull inside.

Ottershaw Park, SW of the village is an Edwardian-Palladian, brick and stone house by Niven and Wigglesworth of 1910, now a County Council boarding school. The wooded grounds screen banal County Council additions and boarding houses, and remains of the 18th-century lodges of the older houses by M. D. Wyatt. Botleys, on the Chertsey Road, is a handsome Palladian stone house of 1765 by Kenton Couse, nicely sited on a little hill, somewhat spoilt by the surrounding mental hospital. At the predecessor of the present freehand-Tudor Anningley Park (1923) lived Thomas Day (1748–89), the author of *Sandford & Merton*.

Outwood [9] A shapeless village on a slight but commanding ridge in the Weald S of Bletchingley, once famous for its old and new windmills working side by side. The younger, a large mid-19th-century weatherboarded smock mill, collapsed in 1961 but the older, dated 1665, a postmill with brick base and tarred weatherboarding top, still survives in good order and may be the oldest working windmill in the country. The church of St John the Baptist is by Wm Burges (1869) in his 13th-

century style. The big stuccoed west tower was added in 1876. Wasp Green farmhouse has a late 17th-century exterior incorporating a 15th-century hall with original tie beam roof.

Oxshott [5] Suburbs in thick pine woods on old commons with mixed woods to the S, mostly owned by the Crown Estate. The church of St Andrew is 1912 Gothic by Caröe and Passmore. Interesting buildings are sadly rare. The best modern houses are two by Powell and Moya (1955) and Wildwood by K. Wood (1959).

Oxted [6] Old Oxted is a medieval, grim-looking, little community of dark brick, half-timbered and tilehung cottages on the steep N slope of the sandy ridge S of the Downs, recently relieved by a short by-pass. The Old Bell Inn at the cross-roads is a 16th-century timber-framed diagonally-braced building, attractive in spite of alterations. New Oxted, off the main road, near the railway station (1884), is quieter and larger. Its shopping centre by the station has early 20th-century half-timbering, which makes Liberty's in London look half-hearted. The rest of new Oxted is 20th-century housing stretching E to Limpsfield and S to Hurst Green. The church of St Mary lies between Old and New Oxted, built in a variety of local stones, Burgate, hearthstone and clunch, partly rebuilt in 1719 and heavily restored in 1877. Its stumpy W tower is 13th-century, it retains 13th- and 14th-century details in the chancel, and has arcades and S doorway of the 15th. The S porch has a moulding with arms of the Cobhams of Lingfield in the spandrels. The E window contains 14th-century glass with symbols of the four evangelists, and four win-

Leith Hill Tower from **Ockley** ▷

dows in the aisle are by Morris and Co. Brasses include a series of the Hoskins family of Barrowgreen Court. St John's at Hurst Green is a neo-Decorated building by J. Oldrid Scott of 1912, enlarged by J. Douglas Matthews in 1962 with a W rose window by J. and M. Kettlewell. Barrow Green Court to the NW is an E-shaped Jacobean house dulled externally by 18th-century alterations but keeping original interiors, while nearby Barrow Green Farm is a 16th-century timber-framed farmhouse.

From the high point on the North Downs are extensive views over the Weald.

Pendell [6] Three fine houses and a farm in a wooded hollow N of Bletchingley. The largest is Pendell Court, a tidy, dull, three-storey building of 1624 still largely Tudor in style, beautifully set in rich trees in the valley bottom. Pendell House, on the N slope, is bright and prominent, dated 1636, and so modern in style as to be ascribed to Inigo Jones. It is a symmetrical, brick building with hipped roof and panels like reversed pilasters on the main elevations. The handsome court-yard walls crested by balls were added in the 18th century. Pendell Manor House, on the southern slope, is a neat brick house of mid-18th-century with an Ionic doorcase.

Peper Harow [7] A mansion with its church and farm in a wooded park sloping SW to the river Wey, W of the Godalming By-pass. The mansion was built for Brodricks by William Chambers in 1763–7. The Brodricks originally lived across the Wey in Oxenford Grange, a grange of

◁ Graffiti of 1700,
Ockley Church

Waverley Abbey till its dissolution in 1536, which was converted to a residence until demolished following the completion of the Peper Harow mansion in 1775. The mansion was altered by the addition of the stone porch (by C. R. Cockerel in 1843) and a third storey and N wing in 1913. The exterior was not one of Chambers's best, and additions made it more lumpish, but the interior has a nicely pilastered entrance hall, an elegant iron staircase and decorated drawing- and dining-rooms. Chambers also built the big quadrangle of stables in brick and Burgate stone, cut to match the brick, and an octagonal dove-cot with lunette pigeon-holes. North of these is the farm, older than the mansion with

Outwood mill

a 17th-century farmhouse and the best farm buildings in Surrey, a quadrangle of 17th- and 18th-century barns and cottages around a 16th-century tilehung and timber-framed granary standing on 25 wooden pillars. The church of St Nicholas is in trees W of the house. The nave walls are old but the tower was added in 1826 and N aisle and chapels added by Pugin in 1843. There is a black marble tablet with two portrait busts of Sir Thomas Brodrick (d 1641) and his wife (d 1678), brought from Wandsworth, and a reclining figure of the Fourth Viscount

◁ The Granary and the entrance to the farm-yard, **Peper Harow**

Oxenford Grange, see **Peper Harow**

Midleton (d 1836) by H. Weeks. Across the river are slight remains of Oxenford Grange, which include a handsome Decorated window in the garden of the 17th-century Oxenford Grange Farmhouse. The nearby stone gatehouse and large barn in 13th-century style were built by Pugin in 1843 to form a picturesque group.

Petersham* [2] The grandest village in Surrey, remarkable for its late 17th- and 18th-century noblemen's houses and for the pre-Victorian fittings of its little church. In the gap between the Thames and the western slope of Richmond Park it is condemned to destruction by through traffic. The chief houses are set close to the narrow main road, often at

sharp bends, so that it is dangerous to stop and admire them. The church is fortunately N of the road, backed by meadows towards Richmond. St Peter's is of brick with arched windows, and has a pretty cupola over a battlemented W tower. The chancel was rebuilt in 1505 and the tiny nave was exploded by the addition of great "transepts" to N and S in the late 18th century and in 1810 respectively. The interior is complete with 18th-century two-decker pulpit, and timber galleries and box pews of pre-Victorian days all beautifully kept. In the chancel is a gaily coloured monument with figures of George Cole (d 1624) and his wife and above its arch are elaborate royal arms as though the church was by royal

Petersham Church

appointment. Captain George Vancouver (d 1798), explorer of the Pacific, is buried in the churchyard. The principal houses are W and S. Petersham House, late 17th century with a domed early 19th-century porch and nice flanking stable buildings, Rutland Lodge, prominent at the corner of River Lane, of 1666 with 18th-century additions, with panelled chimney stacks, and the late 17th-century Montrose House with good iron gates and railings are in a tight group.

Up River Lane are the early 18th-century Manor House with a fine doorcase and the early 18th-

Sudbrook Park, **Petersham**

century Petersham Lodge. The latter has an elaborate elevation to the garden with a central pediment enriched with arms. John Gay often stayed here between 1720 and his death and wrote a great deal in the circular "temple" in the grounds near the river. Captain Vancouver lived between the two at Glen and Craigmyle, then one 17th-century house.

Facing the little avenue which leads W under a neo-Jacobean gate-house leading pedestrians to Ham House is the late 17th-century Douglas House. In Sudbrook Lane are Gort House and Gort Lodge, formerly one, early 18th-century, house and a group of three more fine late 17th-century houses: Sudbrook Cottage of brown brick, Red House of plum brick with red dressings and

Harrington Lodge of brown brick. To the rear is Petersham's second church, All Saints, a very red Italianate of brick terra-cotta by J. Kelly 1907. Sudbrook Lane leads on through a simple pedimented archway with flanking lodges to Sudbrook Park, the grand house built by James Gibbs for the Duke of Argyll in 1726. It was designed for occasional use and consisted principally of the central "cube room" to which access was gained by either of two great Corinthian porticos. This room has a magnificent coved ceiling with cornice supported by Corinthian pilasters and is decorated in a baroque style with trophies.

At 230 Petersham Road, a plain early 18th-century house, Dickens wrote most of *Nicholas Nickleby*.

Pirbright [4] A village round a large green near miles of poor heathlands enjoyed by the army and given comic names like Cowshot and Bullswater Commons. The medieval church of St Michael was rebuilt after fire in a Georgian style of 1785, the present nave and N aisle in red and grey bricks and the tower in ashlar with inset shingled spire. The chancel wall rebuilt in debased Gothic in 1848. Sir H. M. Stanley, the African explorer (d 1904), is buried in the churchyard between over-matured Victorian trees and shrubs under a gigantic block of Dartmoor granite. Pirbright Camp, the Guards' Training Centre, is N of the railway, sheltered in woods of Scots pine, and recently rebuilt with flat roofs and dark bricks by Architects' Co-partnership to

make it the most distinguished camp in the country.

Purley* [6] Decent housing on asphalted downland knotted round the junction of Croydon By-pass and older roads to Brighton and Godstone, three miles S of Croydon. Its parish church, Christ Church, is of 1878. The largest buildings are the Warehousemen's, Clerks' and Drapers' Schools at Russell Hill and the Reedham Orphanage, but the street planting in the garden village estate at Woodcote is more interesting than local buildings.

Puttenham [4] A village of mixed brick, stone, timber and tilehung buildings strung along the "Pilgrim's Way" just S of the Hog's Back. It is on a steep slope and many cottages have to be approached by steps. The church of St John the Baptist is at the E entrance to the village where its 15th-century tower stands like a gatehouse. Most of the nave and chancel is 13th century and the S transept is 14th. The N chapel is 13th, rebuilt in 1770. Woodyer restored the church in 1861 and added the triangular dormer windows on the N side. The base of the arcades rises from bay to bay, suggesting that the early floor stepped upwards. There is a brass of an early 15th-century priest on the chancel floor. The early 19th-century rectory in Tudor style is by J. Perry, and to its SW is Puttenham Priory, a provincial-Palladian house by Thomas Parker of 1762. On the street are Greys Home Farm, 18th century red brick on a stone

◁ Hogs Back landscape, **Puttenham**

Pyrford

base with a range of large black barns ending in four oasthouses, and Winters, 18th century, of stone cut like brick. One mile W is Shoelands, an over-restored brick-faced Tudor house dated 1616, while Rodsall Manor, near the pretty Cutt Mill Ponds, is faced with galletted rubble with red-brick window dressings, dated 1630. There are two later houses of note: Hurlands on the road to Godalming, by P. Webb (1898), and the long, low Greyfriars on the Hog's Back, by C. F. A. Voysey (1896).

Pyrford [3] A church and a few old houses of the medieval village stand isolated on a little hill, overlooking the Wey and ruins of Newark Priory. 20th-century development has spread northwards, pleasantly wooded round Pyrford Common and more densely and bald towards Byfleet. The church of St Nicholas is a rarity in Surrey: an almost unrestored, largely Norman, village church. The walls are of sandstone which have been rendered over. A shingled belfry and broach spire stand over the W end. Inside are a plain Norman font, traces of wall paintings and a pulpit dated 1628 with shaped legs and elaborate sounding board. The E window contains fragments of medieval glass. Pyrford Court nearby is lavish neo-Georgian of 1910, with later additions by Lord Iveagh, who also made the magnificent gardens. Little Court at Pyrford Common was built as "Vodin" by Voysey in 1902, and at Pyrford Green to the NE is the late 17th-century Old House with unusually well-proportioned gauged brick arches, string courses and parapet.

Ranmore

Ranmore

There is a modern church by David Nye (1964) in the 20th-century housing towards Byfleet.

Ranmore [5] A long waving, rough-grass common at the head of the North Downs scarp with clay-based woods sloping gently northward. The southern edge has views over Holmesdale and the Greensand hills to Leith Hill and glimpses of the wider Weald to the SE. A 19th-century settlement centred on Denbies, a large house built for himself by Thomas Cubitt in 1850, on the Downs edge glaring across Dorking in the valley below to its large rival Deepdene. Both have been demolished since World War II. The church, rectory and farm buildings remain. St Bartholomew was built for Cubitt by Sir George Gilbert Scott in 1859, and is one of his best churches with a strong central octagonal tower plus spire and multiple marble shafts and vegetative capitals (in a "certain horrid splendour" to quote the historic building investigator) and black and red font inside.

Redhill [6] A 19th-century town which grew up at the crossing of the E–W route with first the Brighton turnpike (1807) and then the London-Brighton railway (1841). Both followed the nick in the Downs used by the Surrey Iron Railway at Merstham and then the gap in the Greensand hills here. Branch railways went E to Tonbridge in 1842 and W to Guildford in 1849, and the surrounding hills became a popular residence for London businessmen so that it was soon joined to its western neighbour,

Reigate. The principal church, St John, is SW of the town centre on Redhill Common looking S over Earlswood Common and its pretty lakes. It was built in 1843, and largely rebuilt in 1889 by J. L. Pearson, who added the prominent SW tower and spire in 1895. St Matthew's church in Station Road near the centre is a prickly church of 1866, using "firestone" for the body and sandstone for its tower and broach spire. At the cross-roads is a neo-Jacobean Market Hall of 1860, facing the small, disused, market place, for a new market place, with sawn-off 1950–60 shops and flats around, has been built to the SW. NW in Linkfield Road are a few early 19th-century houses, from the hamlet on the widening route which preceded Redhill's turnpike, while on the Brighton Road, S of the town, is the Firs, a bow-windowed, three-storeyed, Regency house with a large extension of 1936 by Basil Ward. The latter was one of the few really modern buildings of that time in Surrey, but has been spoilt by coy additions. At its back is a smaller modern house, the Firkin, by the same architect.

Reigate [6] A residential, medieval market town, set on low sandhills S of the chalk down. It is architecturally disappointing but retains two important buildings, the Church and Reigate Priory, and a historic street pattern with one interesting improvement. The High Street is the old spine of the town running E and W. London Road still enters at its W end, but a dramatic direct entry from the N was made in 1824 by tunnelling under the Castle mount to put visitors right outside the Town Hall. One-way traffic systems have now closed this entry and diverted

traffic from London through the dull neo-Georgian shops of Church Street further E. The parish church, St Mary's, is further E, a large town church first mentioned in the 12th century with nave arcades of that time. The W tower, S porch and chancel chapels were built in the 15th and most of the present detail was renewed in the 19th, part by Woodyer in 1845 and more by Gilbert Scott in 1877, who refaced the tower in Bath stone and rebuilt the noble nave arcades stone by stone. Their capitals with well-carved but still stiff foliage resemble much done at Canterbury. A 15th-century screen embraces both chapels and chancel. Of the monuments, that by J. Rose of Richard Ladbrooke (d 1730) reclining in Roman dress was thought by J. C. Cox "unsuitable for a pagan temple". The great Lord Howard of Effingham is buried (1624) in a vault. Outside is the entrance to an old library over the Tudor vestry and in the churchyard is a local sculptor's 10-foot high obelisk to Baron Masseres (1825). N of the station is St Mark's by Field and Hinton in the sharp Gothic of 1860, while at Dover's Green S of the town is St Peter's, by E. F. Starling (1955), church and hall within one elliptical drum.

Reigate Castle, the mound which shelters the N side of High Street, retains only motte and bailey of the once important castle of the Warrennes, with storage caves now advertised as "dungeons". It was dismantled in 1648 and the site is now a small park on a level with High Street roofs and, with its effusion of roses, seems in summertime out of this world. The "gatehouse" was built from Castle fragments in 1777. The Priory, now a school, was the greatest house in the

town and lies in another part S of High Street. A house of Austin Canons was given by Henry VIII to Lord Howard of Effingham, father of the Armada hero, who built a new house. John Fox, author of the *Book of Martyrs*, was tutor to the family and Archbishop Usher died here (1656). In 1776 the house was rebuilt by Richard Ireland incorporating parts only of the Elizabethan. It is now half-H-shaped facing S, with elevations looking dull late 18th century because of their stucco and in spite of 19th-century embellishment with terra-cotta figures, but inside are two features of great value, the so-called Holbein fireplace in the hall and the staircase. The former is a modest stone fireplace surrounded by a huge timber overmantel with writhing strapwork and Tudor arms and roses. John Evelyn said it was by Holbein and came from Bletchingley but its origin is not yet known.

The staircase was added in the early 18th century. It has beautifully carved twisted and fluted balusters and the staircase well has paintings of classical scenes attributed to Verrio, making the whole the best staircase in the county. The rear courtyard is closed by early 18th-century iron railings and gates which were formerly on the Bell Street entrance. Bell Street itself preserves the pleasant cottagey character of the old road to Brighton before disintegrating round the bus station.

The central feature of the town is the Old Town Hall, built at the cross-roads in 1728 in brick with open, arcaded, ground floor and single room above, approached by an apsed staircase which gives a cheeky rounded look to the High Street. The happy slate lantern, from an adjoining clock tower, was added in 1811. To the E, Church Street, already mentioned, has one nice baroque house of 1721 with cornice, panelled parapet and Corinthian doorcase, known as "Barons" after the eccentric Baron of the Exchequer Masseres, whose monument is in the churchyard.

Further out are two windmills, a postmill on Reigate Heath built in 1765 used as a chapel since 1880, and a tower type on Wray Common of 18th-century tarred brick. Hartswood Manor off Dovers Green Road is a three-storey, much-altered, 17th-century house with some rough plaster pargeting (rare in Surrey) on a gable dated 1615.

Richmond* [2] On a steep slope overlooking a great bend of the Thames, world-famous for its view, and the scene of a favoured royal palace. Bowen, the 18th-century cartographer, called it "the finest village in the British dominions" but traffic and the awful mediocrity of 20th-century building make it another tiresome bottleneck to the average traveller. Bowen's enthusiasm can however be recaptured by turning down the antique-laden lanes to the Green, along the riverside promenade, or, best of all, up to the Terrace Gardens.

The Green first perhaps, for it is the centre of Richmond's royal history. It was the jousting place of the royal palace which stood on the SW side around Old Palace Yard, and was the favourite house of Edward III, who died here in 1377, and of Henry V, who extended it with material from his Byfleet Manor (qv) but it was rebuilt after a fire in knobbly Tudor-style by Henry VII and renamed "Richmond" after his Dukedom in Yorkshire. The village was then called Sheen (cf. East Sheen) but quickly adopted the title of its royal palace. Unfortunately for Surrey it lost favour with subsequent monarchs. Queen Elizabeth I died here (1603) but it then fell into disrepair and in 1649 was sold in ruinous condition into private hands. Only part of a brick gatehouse with the weathered arms of Henry VII on the SW side of the Green and a terrace of 18th-century houses called the Wardrobe, which incorporates a good deal of Tudor brickwork, remain.

To its S is the early 18th-century Trumpeter's House, by John James, with a giant portico of Tuscan columns and pediment facing the river.

The principal building now facing the Green is a three-storeyed terrace of houses, set behind iron gates and railings on the SW side, known as Maid of Honour Row, which was built (1724) for the household of Caroline of Anspach, who was living at Richmond Lodge (now vanished) in the Deer Park. The houses are of five bays all with good doorcases and they have fine interiors, but they are rarely seen to advantage for their Green side is usually in shadow which looks gloomy, even ill-proportioned, in silhouette. The N side has mid-19th-century Italianate houses, and a dark-brick, three-storey terrace by Manning and Clamp 1968, too neat and small for the generous scale of the Green. Facing the adjoining little Green is the red brick and brown terra-cotta-faced Theatre, with twin turrets and copper cupolas like a stray from Leicester Square, by F. Machin (1899), and a Gothic public library by F. S. Brunton (1880). The SE side of the Green is filled with large 18th-century houses and little lanes full of curios which lead back to the large shops in George Street and across the latter to the church.

St Mary Magdalene is hemmed by grim commercial buildings off the southern loop of the one-way traffic stream. Of the medieval church only a 15th-century stone and flint W tower remains, largely rebuilt in 1624. The N aisle was rebuilt in brick in 1699 and the nave and S aisle in 1750 in red and yellow brick, with a pediment centrally over the S side which makes this side look like an orangery. The chancel and chapels were rebuilt in 1904 by G. F. Bodley, who also designed the stained glass. Inside are an 18th-century pulpit, and fluted bowl font of the same period and a number of 17th-, 18th- and 19th-century monuments, e.g. the medallions to Edmund Kean, the actor (d 1833), who lived at the Green, and another to James Thomson (d 1748), poet author of The Seasons. In the crowded churchyard is a memorial to Viscount Fitzwilliam (d 1816), founder of the Cambridge museum, and Scheemeker's sarcophagus and obelisk to Sir Mathew Decker (1759).

The most imposing church in the town is, however, G. G. Scott's St Matthias in Friars Stile Road on high ground to the SE, built 1858 with a tall spire on NW tower.

From the W the only entry to the town is over Richmond Bridge, of five beautiful stone arches, by James Paine (1777), spoilt by widening and flattening of its original peaked carriageway.

The bridge is flanked triumphantly by the 1840 campanile of Willoughby House.

Opposite Bridge Street in Ormond Road is an exceptional group of early 18th-century houses. The Vineyard running parallel a little S has three sets of almshouses: Michel's founded 1659, rebuilt 1811, Bishop

Duppa's founded 1661 and re-built here in Victorian Jacobean by T. Little (1850), and Queen Elizabeth's, rebuilt in 1767.

Richmond Hill starts from the town end of the Vineyard and rises to reveal first Cardigan House, home of the commander of the Light Brigade, now part of the British Legion's poppy factory, and then the Terrace Gardens. They stretch down the Hill across Petersham Road to the riverside site of Buccleugh House, whose gardens they once were.

Richmond

◁ Duppa's almshouses and St Mary Magdalene Churchyard

(*this page*) Domestic details

Trumpeter's House, Richmond

The famous view can be seen best from inside the gardens on the grass slopes. In the foreground is the bend of the Thames between Ham and Richmond with little Glover's Island in the middle, between the maturely wooded grounds of Marble Hill, Twickenham, and Ham House. Beyond, it runs over apparently endless woods to the North Downs and Windsor Castle, on the skyline. There is little sign of the thousands of people who live within the arc of view and, apart from being a beautifully com-posed view, it preserves with the care of trees and parks the most precious illusion in the London area.

The road continues to Richmond Park and while views diminish architectural interest increases. On the W are The Wick by Robert Mylne, 1775, which has an oval drawing-room on the first floor framing the Thames within the segmental bay which runs the full height of the house and, next door, Wick House built for Sir Joshua Reynolds by Sir William Chambers (1772) in brown brick unkindly immured in 19th-century cement. On the E side is a varied range of 18th- and early 19th-century buildings. Opposite and dominating many views of the Hill, but luckily not that from the Terrace Gardens, is the elephantine, neo-Georgian, Star and Garter Home for ex-service men built in 1924 by Sir Edwin Cooper. Richmond Park beyond, partly in Barnes, Ham and Kingston parishes, is the largest enclosed public open space in Greater London, nearly four square miles in extent. It was enclosed with a high wall 11 miles long and stocked with deer by Charles I in 1637 and it remained a royal hunting ground until the 18th century. The Park still contains herds of fallow and red deer and can be well seen from the single motor-road round the perimeter, though the ponds in the centre can only be reached on foot. Of buildings within the Park, White Lodge (in Barnes parish), a fine ashlar house started in 1728 by the Earl of Pembroke as a hunting lodge for George II with quadrant wings added in mid-18th-century was the birthplace of the Duke of Windsor (1894) and is now a ballet school. Thatched House Lodge to the S (in Kingston parish) was built for Sir Robert

Walpole in the early 18th century while the Thatched House is a summer house in its garden with rooms painted by Angelica Kauffman. Pembroke Lodge (in Petersham parish) is 18th century and was occupied by Lord Macaulay (d 1859) and by Lord John Russell (d 1878).

Return from the Star and Garter Home can be made on foot past the jolly Victorian vulgarity of the Star and Garter Hotel (1874), along the tow-path through the pretty Buccleugh Gardens, under the Bridge, and past Trumpeter's House up to the noisy railway bridge. Before this is Asgill House, built by Sir Robert Taylor (1770), restored by D. Insall in 1970. Its big canted bays disguise the octagonal plan based on one of the bastions of the medieval palace. The eaves are deep and boldly detailed, and the house has a fiercely chiselled look. The upper floor has an octagonal room on the river front with wall paintings by A. Casali.

N of the railway is the bridge carrying the "new" Twickenham road over the river completed 1933 to the design of Maxwell Ayrton. Across the road in Richmond Old Deer Park is the site of Richmond Lodge (see Kew), the town's modern swimming baths, by Leslie Gooday (1964) in grey-brown brick with copper roofs and, to the N, the stands of the Rugby Club by Manning and Clamp overlooked by the Pagoda at the southern end of Kew Gardens. Lucky Richmond to have such royal open spaces and the river to link them.

Ripley [5] A coaching village on the London–Portsmouth road with a gently curved street and glimpses of a large green widening out to the N. The parish church of St Mary, near the centre,

Asgill House, **Richmond**

was only a chapel of ease to Send until 1878 and of little obvious interest, though the chancel is late 12th century. The nave is by B. Ferrey (1846). The High Street is made up of varied and attractive buildings, the best being old coaching inns, including the half-timbered rambling Anchor Hotel. Tudor House and Cedar House, formerly the George Inn, a 16th- and 17th-century three-storeyed, timber-framed building with painted brick infilling, and elaborate 18th-century doorways. The Talbot Hotel is 17th century,

refronted in the 18th. The Manor House, opposite the Anchor, is a Dutch-gabled building dated 1650.

Ripley Court School in Rose Lane is also 17th century refronted in early 18th century. Alone in the fields a mile N and almost surrounded by the Wey, are the romantic ruins of Newark Priory, a house of Austin Canons founded in the 12th century and dissolved in 1538. The present remains are the Priory church, principally the S transept and parts of the choir and presbytery. It had chapels of varied length running E from the S transept while the "crossing" was blocked by ten-foot walls on the N and S so that the transepts were cut off from the choir. There is hardly a dressed stone left today. Towards Send Marsh is Papercourt Farm, a picturesque, though restored, red-brick Manor House of the late 16th century.

Sanderstead* [6] Village pond and church at the central crossroads still look villagey, though many square miles of dull suburban housing obliterates the downland around them. All Saints is largely 11–13th centuries with cement-rendered walls and weatherboarded steeple. Inside are 14th-century wall paintings (elongated figures of King Edward the Martyr and St Edmund of Canterbury), a 16th-century brass, a hanging monument of 1600 and a shrouded effigy of 1655. In Limpsfield Road, beyond the usual 20th-century shopping parade, are the late 17th-century yellow- and red-brick Old Rectory and 16th-century timber-framed White House.

Sandhills [7] Largely 19th-century houses but with some old cottages strung along a sandy ridge SW of Witley. There are

two notable late 19th-century houses, Kingwood by F. W. Troup and Barnacle Edge by Basil Champneys set to enjoy the wide southward view.

Seale [4] A compact little village in a well-treed hollow south of the Hog's Back. The church of St Lawrence at its centre is picturesque, cruciform and blunt with central tower and pyramidal spire, N aisle and S porch. The last is 14th-century timber-framed; otherwise the building is by J. Croft (1873). There are monuments to Anne Woodroffe (1762), with a rococo tablet, and to E. N. Long (1809), with a relief of a naval accident. The deep disused chalk quarry NE of the village is a botanical reserve of the Surrey Naturalists' Trust.

Selsdon* [6] Selsdon adjoins Sanderstead and like the latter is largely modern suburbia on downland. St John's church with square tower and lancet windows by Newberry and Fowler (1936) is red brick outside and cream brick inside. 19th- and 20th-century addition to Selsdon Park Hotel hides a 15th-century half-H-plan house. The adjoining beechy Selsdon Wood is a bird reserve (NT).

Send [5] A large, badly treated, village which is mainly 20th-century sprawl around the Woking–Clandon Road. The church with one large house and a farm is isolated by acres of old gravel pits to the SW. St Mary's has a 13th-century chancel with lancets to N and S but a geometric E window of 1819, a Perpendicular 14th-century nave with 17th-century W gallery and a Perpendicular screen (badly restored), a timber-framed 15th-century S porch and a Perpen-

dicular W tower. Send Grove House, adjoining, is large plain late 18th century. It has an 18th-century stable block with wooden bell cupola and roundheaded rusticated coachhouse doors and pedimented gables. Send Court farmhouse is an early 17th-century timber-framed T-shaped building. At Send Marsh to the NE of the main village is the Manor House, a well-proportioned three-storey, red-brick 17th-century house facing a tiny green and more 20th-century sprawl.

Shackleford [7] A pleasant village NW of Godalming. Victorian growth on the sandy southern fringe was given a church by G. G. Scott in 1865, early English in style, of Burgate stone, well-proportioned, and one of his best. Near the church Voysey built a big house, Norney, in 1897, using rough-cast and yellow limestone. The main street trickles NW from this to the old village proper, past Aldro School, which retains stables of 1743, built in stone cut as bricks and capped by a bell cupola, and between over-restored cottages. Adjoining the Old Cottage are well-known brick "crinkle-crankle" walls in continuous bows.

Shalford [4] Refurbished half-timbered cottages, straggling S from the expensive suburbs of Guildford, to the more plebeian 19th-century houses of Shalford Common. The Church of St Mary was rebuilt by B. Ferrey (1846) in 13th-century style. There is stained glass in the E window by R. Morrow and a few 18th-century tablets from the older church. Shalford House, the only large house in the village, is stuccoed late 18th century but incorporates an older house, home of one family, the Austens, from 1599 to early 20th century. On the Tillingbourne, E of the village street, is Shalford Mill, a pretty three-storey building and its attractive 17th-century timber-framed mill house.

The medieval fair, which may have suggested Vanity Fair to Bunyan, was held in meadows to the N.

Shamley Green [8] A pleasant village set about a triangular green W of the high Greensand hills, SE of Bramley, with old "improved" cottages and indifferent but secluded bungalows. Christchurch is a stone chapel by C. H. Howell of 1864.

Shepperton** [2] Old Shepperton is a small, sheltered village by the river; modern Shepperton a dull suburb to the N. The tiny square with the church at its E end and pubs to N and S is one of the best village scenes in Middlesex (or Surrey), but to enjoy it one must turn one's back on the petrol station and busy road to Staines on the W. The church of St Nicholas was rebuilt in 1614, following a disastrous flood, with much of the flint rubble and Reigate stone dressings from the 12th-century church. Unfortunately all the old detail has gone. The most notable external feature is the oblong W tower in brick rebuilt (once again) in 1710. The whole church was restored in 1934 when vestries were added to the SE. It has a simple cross-shaped plan with substantial transepts, early 19th-century fittings, gallery at the W end, another in the N transept supported by slender iron pillars, and a whole set of box pews which give the church a particularly homely and welcoming look.

Just N stands the Rectory, a large house handsomely refronted in seven bays of brick in the early 18th century, hiding the timber frame of a 15th-century hall behind. The view of the 18th-century front from the Square has recently been marred by the addition of a detached brick garage. On the S side of the Square are the pleasant 19th-century fronts of Warren Lodge, Thomas House and the King's Head pub and beyond, behind the church, are views of a bend in the Thames and the wall of the Manor House, a stuccoed house with verandahs of about 1830. There are views of this and its fine lawns from the river and Surrey bank.

Church Road contains a few old cottages, and leads towards modern Shepperton which spread its suburban semis hugely round the railway, which reached here in 1864, but luckily never reaching the old village.

On the Walton road, along the river front beyond, lies Lower Halliford where Thomas Love Peacock and his son-in-law George Meredith lived at Elm Bank.

The Shepperton Film Studios are in Littleton, qv. J. M. Neale the hymn writer, was vicar here and wrote an historical romance *Shepperton Manor* (1844) which has the old village as its setting. (The "Shepperton" of George Eliot's *Scenes from Clerical Life* is based on a village in Warwickshire.)

Shere [5] The most photographed and (though overpraised) probably most attractive village in Surrey, sited on the Tillingbourne between Downs and Greensand hills. It has an H plan: Church Square and Lower Street along the river, Upper Street along the Guildford Road at the top and High Street joining them to views of hills at each end. The church of St James is approached off Lower Street, via timber and plaster cottages around Church Square, and entered through a Lutyens lych gate, past a Lutyens war memorial. It is heavy-looking 13th century with big roofs, central Norman tower and big shingled broach spire. The plan is Norman and there is a Norman S door with two orders of zigzag chevrons and foliage. The S aisle was extended in the mid-13th century to form a chapel, and a cell for an anchoress was added to the chancel in 1329. Only the quatrefoil and squint apertures that once linked this insanitary addition remain. In the 14th century the chapel of St Nicholas was built between buttresses N of the crossing, the chancel was extended to an E window with four quatrefoils in a roundel supported on an ogee-headed arch, the E and W crossing arches were rebuilt and the spire was built. The W gallery was added in 1748. The church was brightly restored by Louis Osman in 1957. The S or Bray chapel, named after the family who have been Lords of the Manor since 1487, has a memorial to William Bray (d 1832), joint author of Manning and Bray's *History and Antiquities of Surrey* 1804–14 and, in the 13th-century stained glass of the E window, symbolic figures of the four evangelists. There is more 13th-century glass in the E window of the chancel. There are brasses to Robert Scarcliff, rector (d 1412), and to John Touchet, Lord Audley (d 1491), a figure in armour 20 inches high, and a 13th-century font of Purbeck marble. There are old cottages in all the village streets, not individually outstanding but prettily grouped particularly near the river and in Upper Street. To the NE is the heavy classical Netley House of 1851 in parkland running up to wooded downs.

Shere

Shirley* [3] An eastern suburb of Croydon. The church of St John is a large flint and stone church with a spired belfrey-turret by Sir Giles Gilbert Scott, 1856. John Ruskin's parents are buried in the churchyard under his epitaph for them. The Shirley poppy was first grown here by one of its vicars.

A tarred brick windmill is in the grounds of the John Ruskin grammar school (by Paul Mauger,) and in Addiscombe Road are new buildings, by George Lowe, of the Trinity School of John Whitgift, which moved here from Croydon, 1965.

For Slyfield *see* Fetcham.

Staines* [2] Though an important bridge-head over the Thames from Roman times, Staines remained a quiet country town until this century; its population was only 6,000 in 1901, and its rapid growth to the wide, solidly built-up area of today began in the early motor era, for while the railway came through on its way to Windsor in 1848 it caused no violent changes outside the local impact of its ugly iron bridge on the river. Much of the country-town character can still be found near the church and even on the main road from the bridge to the Market Place further E. The most important building, the parish church of St Mary, is disappointing. Its best feature is the brick W tower of 1631, heightened in 1828 when the rest of the church was completely rebuilt, dully in yellow stock brick, by J. B. Watson. The tower is ascribed, by a stone of 1791 set in the S wall, to Inigo Jones. Most of the older buildings in the town are still clustered in Church Street, whose western end is dignified Georgian, but a few others have survived to the E in the High Street. Here is the Blue Anchor Hotel, a coaching house refronted in chequered brick about 1700 and altered internally in the 18th century, when two good staircases and internal panelling were added.

The present road bridge across the Thames has three graceful segmental granite arches with cutwaters running under their springing courses. Built by George Rennie in 1829–32, it was the fourth bridge to be built here within 30 years. Two predecessors of iron collapsed almost as soon as completed. Traces of a stone abutment of the earlier bridge can be seen downstream from Rennie's bridge opposite the Italianate Town Hall of 1880.

Upstream and W of the church is a small riverside park. Here imprisoned in municipal railings is the medieval London Stone which from 1285 marked the upstream limit of jurisdiction over the Thames of the City of London. It stands on a pedestal of 1781 and is badly worn, but was the subject of many civic visits by dignitaries of the City, and it still marks the boundary between the upper and lower Thames and between the new Surrey and Buckinghamshire.

North of the town centre are the works of the former Linoleum Manufacturing Company, the largest lino works in the world. Then comes the by-pass of 1961

(extended to Ashford in 1964) and N of this three large reservoirs of the Metropolitan Water Board whose high, grassed, banks cropped by sheep give an occasional illusion of rural life. Most of the land around is filled with inter- and post-war bungalows.

There are surprisingly few good modern buildings in this flourishing town. Better than average are the offices of United Glass in Kingston Road, by T. G. Crossgrove (1965) and two sets of six linked houses in Riverside Road by Broadway and Malyan (1968).

Stanwell** [2] This medieval village lies NE of Staines between the four great reservoirs on Staines and Stanwell moors and the prairie of London Airport, which makes the place one of roaring restlessness. Most of the area is indeterminate suburban housing but there is still a little triangular medieval green with the church at the S end, some Georgian brick houses to the W and N and a few older timbered cottages just N of these. The chief feature of the church of St Mary is the 13th- and 14th-century nicely-patterned flint tower with its shingled spire. The walls are of flint and stone rubble with Reigate and other freestone dressings. Inside, the nave arcades of 1260 have alternating octagonal and circular piers, while the tower arches date from the end of the century. Much of the chancel is of the 14th century, where the elaborate arcading on the S side is continued to form sedilia in which every curve is an ogee. The S aisle is later 14th century and retains figured corbels of that date. Against the N wall of the chancel and cutting into its arcading is the church's

chief monument, to Lord and Lady Knyvett, who died in 1622. It was Knyvett who arrested Guy Fawkes in the vaults of Parliament. They are portrayed in more-than-life-size kneeling marble figures by Nicholas Stone, set between black marble columns with alabaster curtains under a broken segmental pediment.

To the E of the old village in Bedfont Road stands another monument to Lord Knyvett, the Free School founded under his will in 1624. This is a simple two-storey brick building containing the school house (one high room) on the left and the schoolmaster's house on the right. It has recently been converted into two private houses. It is larger than the original Harrow school of 1611 and has been less altered externally.

Further E along Bedfont Road there is a view (obstructed by crude fencing and lined with the concrete drain into which the historic Longford River was diverted to extend the airport) of London's major airport and the new cargo buildings on its southern fringe. Here are the British Airways "Cargo-Centre" by Gollins, Melvin and Ward (1966), a barrel-vaulted boiler house by Frederick Gibberd and Partners (1967), and the Airport Authority's cargo buildings by Yorke, Rosenberg and Mardell (1968)—all worth a look.

Nicholas Hilliard, the Elizabethan miniaturist, lived at Poyle, to the N of Stanwell, and the Cox's Orange Pippin apple was first grown (1845) on the Bath Road on the Stanwell side of Colnbrook.

Stoke D'Abernon [5] A church and manor house, isolated by playing fields from the suburban area of the same name which stretches from the railway station N to Cobham and Oxshott. The church is world famous for its memorial brasses, the oldest surviving in this country. St Mary's, by the river Mole, is approached by a chestnut avenue which also serves the Manor House. Restorations have given it a hard Victorian look and taken away its feeling of history which goes back to 7th century. Nave and chancel show Roman bricks and traces of Saxon apse. The N aisle was added in the early 12th century and in the early 13th the Saxon apse was enlarged into a two-bay, rib-vaulted, square-ended chancel. The Perpendicular style N chapel dated about 1490, by Sir John Norbury, as a thank-offering for victory at Bosworth is divided from the chancel by a panelled arch, remains of the original monument to Sir John, and contains a contemporary fireplace. A later monument to him in anachronistic Carolean armour was erected on its E wall in 1633. The rest of the church was messed about by Ford and Hesketh in 1866. The early Saxon chancel arch was removed, the mean N tower and S aisle added and the W end extended. The interior is still rich in fittings. Two great monumental brasses are on the chancel floor, to Sir John D'Abernon (1277), six feet six inches long, with Sir John in chain mail and surcoat, his feet resting comfortably on a small lion, which is nibbling his lance. The brass is the oldest surviving in the country and unique in showing a lance. His son, also Sir John (1327), is alongside. Here the figure set under ogee canopy is only five feet long and wears a combination of chain mail and plate armour with a cyclas. There are smaller, later, brasses to Anne Norbury (d 1469) with eight

children in folds of her gown, and Ellen Bray in chrisom (1516), on the ends of the Norbury tomb. Also in the Norbury chapel are monuments to Sarah, wife of Sir Francis Vincent (d 1608), and to Sir Thomas Vincent (d 1613) and his wife, which have life-size effigies under crested canopies. On the S wall of the church is a tablet to Thomas Lyfelde of 1592 and his wife (a Bray) and daughter who married a Vincent, with a genealogical tree in brass tracing the descent of the Vincent family from the D'Abernons through five families. The late Elizabethan pulpit supported on seven carved monsters, has a sounding board suspended on elaborate wrought-iron ties. The windows were filled in mid-20th century with a remarkable collection of old glass: the E window with 15th-century Rhenish glass brought from Norfolk, the chancel lancets with 15th-century English panels and 16th-century roundels and the N transept with 16th-century panels and some older English quarries. In the Norbury Chapel are a series of 17th-century heraldic shields of the D'Abernon and Vincent families, and seven 16th-century Flemish medallions. The Manor House, by the river next to the church on Roman villa site contains fragments of the Vincents' house but is mainly late 18th century. Motorway M25 will pass on a high bank just S of the Manor House.

Sunbury on Thames** [2] Old Sunbury is a curved ribbon of historic houses and trees along the Thames. New is centred on the clock tower at Sunbury Cross to the N, dissected by the Staines–Kingston Road, the railway and the Basingstoke motorway. Otherwise it consists almost entirely of inter-war

development of little interest. The parish church of St Mary stands in the old village on a slight mound which was the centre of prehistoric settlement. Its best overall view is from the Surrey bank of the Thames. The W tower is part of a modest church designed by S. Wright in 1752, and improved by S. S. Teulon in 1862, who added a heavily decorated chancel. This was greatly enlarged in 1971 on a new axis retaining Teulon's chancel as a side chapel.

Sunbury Court, the major historic house in Sunbury, lies about a quarter of a mile downstream. It is of seven bays in red brick with stone dressings and a central pediment carried on Ionic pilasters. Most dates from 1770. In the saloon are contemporary (late 18th century) paintings by the Swedish painter Elias Martin. Other houses of note are the 18th-century Wilmary, Darby House and Orchard House along the river front, and Hawke House (dated 1703), which was the home of Admiral Hawke, and the 17th-century Three Fishes public house in Green Street. Anthony Trollope was a pupil of a private school here for some time after leaving Harrow.

The growth of the main modern centre at Sunbury Common began with the advent of the railway in 1864 but its most rapid expansion was in the inter-war years. Post-war years have added slightly better-than-average tower flats and the Surrey County Architect's Central Library, neatly filling a gap in the suburban shopping parade.

To the east lies Kempton Park, a popular racecourse in attractive parkland, now like so much more in Middlesex, being scarred for gravel.

Further E and to the N are

numerous reservoirs of the Metropolitan Water Board with pump houses in styles from high Victorian Italianate to modern cinematic.

At Charlton, a curiously isolated hamlet further N, the thatched Harrow Inn dates back to 1500.

Sunningdale [1] The commercial, railway station, end of Sunningdale (Berkshire).

Surbiton* [2] Was already a southern suburb of Kingston when the Southampton railway was built in 1838 and the first station was called "Kingston". New housing sprang up near the station and spread generously over low hills to the S. The town has a number of Victorian churches. St Andrew's in Maple Road is by Sir A. Blomfield, 1871, in yellow and red brick with a detached N tower; St Mark's in St Mark's Hill, has a tower by P. C. Hardwick 1855, and a body rebuilt after war damage by Milner and Craze, and Christ Church in King Charles' Road in brick with stone dressings is by C. L. Luck, mostly 1863 but extended later. Luck also built in 1874 the most imposing of all Surbiton churches, St Matthew's, which has a prominent SW tower and spire, on Ewell Road S of the town. St Raphael's, the R.C. church in Portsmouth Road, is of 1847 by Charles Parker (who made a copy of it at St Alban's), in an ambiguous Italian style with a W tower which is a landmark on the river frontage. In Ashcombe Avenue, one of many tree-lined roads S of the railway, is Southborough House, medium-sized, L-shaped and stuccoed with a domed porch, by John Nash 1808, and the only notable

building of this date in the town. The railway station, now named "Surbiton", for a more direct line to Kingston was built in 1863, was rebuilt in 1937 by J. R. Scott. It was the first outside the underground system in a modern style in Britain. At Surbiton Common was fought the last Battle of the Civil War (1648).

Sutton* [6] A small village in the 19th century but now an endless suburb of London created by its Victorian railway system; like many places in mid-Surrey it has developed with small houses on the clay to the N and larger houses and gardens on the sands and chalk towards the Downs. There is still some rough downland Common just S of the town, but little of the village or sign of its history left. The medieval church of St Nicholas W of the High Street was rebuilt by Edwin Nash in flint with a broach spire in 1862. In its churchyard is the pyramidal mausoleum of the Gibson family of 1777, opened each August to ensure that bodysnatchers have not rifled the tombs. In Cheam Road are the Trinity (Methodist) church by Gordon and Gunton, 1907, which has a prominent tower crowned like that of Newcastle Cathedral, and a large brick Baptist church by Welch, Cachemaile Day and Lauder (1934) in the modern style of that day. Of the other churches, All Saints in Benhilton Road by S. S. Teulon, 1865, is large and straightforward, and Christ Church in the copper-beech-lined Christ Church Park, by Newman and Jacques, 1888, has a rood screen in which the rood is carried on an openwork crown. The town centre is a smaller version of Croydon with busy ugly shops and a collection of tall office blocks. There are two by Owen Luder in chunky rough concrete (Eagle Star House of 1967 and the

eleven-storey Civic Offices of 1963), and smoother blocks by the station, eg the seventeen-storey Vigilant House by Robert Wood, 1966, but the most attractive new building is a shop front in steel and glass for the display of furniture for Amos Reynolds by Michel Manser (1966).

Sutton Place [4] A large Tudor house in the southern part of the parish of Woking in a wide bow of the river Wey, built in the early 1520s by Sir Richard Weston (d 1542), it is the finest house of its period in Surrey and of national interest for it is one of the first to pay no attention to its defence and to show marked Italian influence in its design. The two-storeyed brick building with long projecting wings ending in stepped gables was originally quadrangular with an entrance range on the NE which had a central, 70 feet high, turreted gatehouse reminiscent of Hampton Court, demolished in 1786. Sir Richard was a favourite of Henry VIII, although his son was executed during the Boleyn scandals. He travelled on many diplomatic missions and was much taken by Italian building of that time. His house is remarkable for the symmetry of its design and for the widespread and early use of terracotta and particularly for the repeated use of standard naked "amorini" as decoration. There is a panel of twelve of them above the rather mean central N door in the S range. This door leads straight into the Great Hall, 51 feet long and nearly 31 feet high. The present plaster ceiling conceals the original beams and the Hall has been much altered, but its glass contains a remarkable collection of painted shields of royal and family arms, a large group dating from the early 16th century, another from the mid-17th century

and a third from various ages down to the mid-19th. The finest single room is the long gallery on the upper floor of the SE range, which is 152 feet long and 22 feet wide, although the detail dates from the Norman Shaw restoration. The house was the English home of the late American Paul Getty. The Wey nearby is by-passed by the Wey Navigation constructed in 1651–53 with Dutch type locks by a later Richard Weston of Sutton Place.

Sutton Place

The centre of the north front (*right*) and details of the terracotta work

Tadworth [5] Twentieth-century downland sprawl round a railway station on the way to Epsom Downs but not unpleasing thanks to the Surrey passion for trees and gardening. There are two items of architectural interest, Tadworth Court, near the Brighton Road, a late 17th-century house in yellow brick, with stone dressings, with handsome entrance front leading to a rococo-plastered two-storey hall, and the UOP factory, to the N, in primrose GRP panels by Piano and Rogers (1974).

Tandridge [6] A village on the isolated sandy hill SW of Oxted flanked by a golf-course. The church of St Peter lies on the W side. The body is 12th and 13th century. Its modern belfry is supported on big medieval timbers with irregular cross bracing. Aisles were added in the 19th century, the N in 1874 by Sir Giles Gilbert Scott, who lived at Rooksnest on the boundary of Godstone qv. He designed the reredos and, in the churchyard, the marble tomb of Lady Scott (d 1872). The parish is rich in old Wealden farmhouses. Two of the best are on the lane S to Lingfield, Hobbs Farmhouse with a 17th-century front hiding a 15th-century rear, Horsham slate roofs and big brick chimneystacks and Brook Farmhouse, red brick, mid-18th century.

Tatsfield [6] High on the North Downs at the Kent border is this early 20th-century shack colony, now clothed with trees and shrubs, and as pleasant as Welwyn Garden City. The parish church of St Mary is isolated in beech trees on the crest and at 788 feet above sea level is the highest church in the county. It is not otherwise distinguished except by the view S from its churchyard. The nave walls are Norman in dark and light sandstone, the chancel is largely 13th century and the little tower set in the nave is of 1838. The lancet window at the NE end of the nave has elaborate mouldings, unexpected in so plain a church.

Thames Ditton [2] Once a fine Thames-side village. The High Street still leads to the river between the parish church and grand brick walls of its chief house, now a children's home, but gives only a glimpse of a backwater. The church of St Nicholas in flint and stone is low and broader than long, but the view from the High Street of its four gable ends and the 13th-century W tower capped with weatherboarded belfry and spiky spire is the best in the village. There are fragments of the 13th and earlier centuries but most has been so altered as to leave few early details. Inside are a Norman font with crude symbolic carvings, one of a goat falling on its horns, a canopied tomb of Erasmus Forde (d 1533), which looks as though it had re-used part of the Easter Sepulchre nearby, brasses of the early 16th century, wall monument to Sidney Godolphin (1732), and above the chancel arch, painted panels of Judgment Day. Opposite is the big three-storey red-brick house, now a children's home, with its pedimented centre and modillion cornice, 18th century refronted in the early 20th, with a two-storey yellow-brick stable block adjoining, impressively blocking one long side of the street. At the N end of High Street is the 16th-century Swan Inn and a group of white-washed houses. Other good buildings such as the Bridges Almshouses of 1720 are scattered down Station Road towards Weston Green.

Thornton Heath* [3] North of Croydon. Mostly terrace houses which filled the gap between Croydon and Norwood following the railway's arrival in the 19th century. St Alban's in Grange Road is a large church by Bucknall and N. Comper 1889–94, in red brick, Perpendicular style. Almost dull inside as little of Comper's interior detail was carried out.

Thorpe [2] The village centre has high curving brick walls shielding small country houses in small parks, as Thames Ditton was once, not now found elsewhere in Surrey, but its fields have been cut up by great wet gravel pits, "restored" areas turned to scruffy industrial sites and interstices filled with bungalows. Through the gaps two motorways are now threaded, making it the most badly treated village in the county. The church of St Mary is down a lane behind more curved walls. Parts are of 12th century, including the plain chancel arch, but most is now 19th-century rebuilding with a few Decorated details. The brick tower is late 16th century. Inside are 14th-century piscina and sedilia with ogee heads, and an early work of Sir Robert Taylor, the monument to Elizabeth Townsend (d 1754) with praying cherub. The best house is Thorpe House (crowded with thoughtless bungalows), 17th century with 18th-century front in stock brick and red-brick dressings, and giant Doric pilasters in moulded brick on the end bays. Spelthorne St Mary (now a Roman Catholic home), a dull late 18th-century house, has early 18th-century wrought-iron gates brought here from Feltham.

Tadworth Court ▷

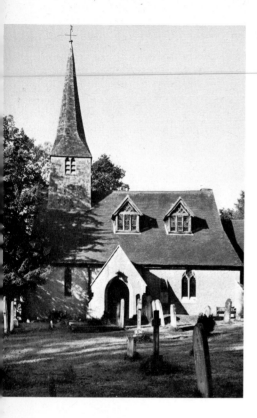

Tandridge

Thursley [7] A centre of medieval glass and iron industry, now a fossilised picturesque village between heathy commons which extend S to include Gibbet Hill and the Devil's Punch Bowl. A little road to Churt crosses a narrow green surrounded by old cottages at the N end of the village but the best part is up the winding street towards the spired church. St Michael's has a Saxon body with two tiny Saxon windows with oak frames that once held horn windows and a Saxon oven in the chancel, but overall it looks crude Early English, thanks to brutal 19th-century alterations by B. Ferrey (1860), who added the N aisle and J. Penfold (1884) who added the S porch and S transept. The timber belfry and octagonal

spire were added in the late 15th century and provide the most dramatic incident of the interior for they are carried from the centre of the nave on a cage of unnecessarily massive moulded oak piers linked with stout tie-beams to arched braces taking up a lot of space. The tub font with crude chevron band is 11th century. In the N aisle is 15th-century Flemish glass brought from Costessy (cf. Stoke D'Abernon). The poet John Freeman (1880–1929) is buried in the churchyard and the adjoining field is a memorial to him. There is also a crude memorial to the sailor killed by companions at Hindhead in 1786. Near the church are the late 17th-century half H-shaped Hilldown, with symmetrical brick front, and the 16th-century Old Parsonage, half-timbered with brick filling. There are small groups of pretty cottages, in timber, stone or brick with or without tilehanging, down the street. Sir Edwin Lutyens, the best-known Surrey architect (1869–1944), was born at the Cottage (now Lutyens House) near the Green. A pseudacacia on the Green was planted in memory of Cobbett, who often stayed here and encouraged the extensive planting of this American tree on poor soils in southern England. On the damper parts of Thursley Common around hammer ponds to the E is a large nature reserve. The ponds worked iron forges until the late 18th century and damage to the Portsmouth Road by the carriage of their products was a constant source of complaint.

Tilford [7] An outspread village in folded, sandy, wooded country at the junction of the two arms of the river Wey. The visual centre is the large triangular green connected to the rest of the village by two medieval bridges. That to the

E has five stone arches and a later brick arch, and was probably built by monks from Waverley Abbey which lay only a mile NW. Its first church, now a school, was built in 1857 on the green. The second, All Saints, was built nearby in late 13th-century style against a background of pine trees in Burgate stone, by E. Christian in 1867. A Bach festival is held there each spring. Most of the village is E of the green but the chief house, Tilford House, is NW. This is early 18th-century, two-storeyed, red brick, similar to the best in Farnham. The central bay has a tiny pediment and the doorcase contains a sundial. Its front garden is enclosed by contemporary serpentine walls in red brick and sandstone cut like brick, with double Chinese-Chippendale-pattern wooden gates. The outbuilding to the SE was built as a Presbyterian Chapel in 1776. Crooksbury Hill is a conical, sandy hill which forms a popular picnic spot 1½ miles N of the village. On its S slope is Crooksbury House (or Lodge), Lutyens' first country house, the earliest part in half-timber and tilehanging dating from 1890 but with additions of 1898 and 1914 in Queen Anne and Tudor style, which Lutyens himself came to regret.

Titsey [6] The tiny estate village of Titsey Park, at the foot of a wooded spur jutting S from a high point on the North Downs. The church of St James was built by J. L. Pearson in 1861 in harsh Victorian and contains 14th-century encaustic tiles, coffin slabs and a monument to Sir John Gresham (d 1643) from the old church in the park removed by the Greshams in 1776 to make way for their house. The latter is a two-storeyed building with early 19th-century stucco and Gothic details. A Roman villa, later converted to

Thursley

fulling works, was unearthed in the Park in 1864 and a Romano-Celtic temple of the third century was discovered one mile E of Titsey in 1879.

Tolworth* [2] Endless semis fringing the Kingston By-pass, now given a focal point by Tolworth Tower, a 22-storey office slab on splayed stilts by R. Seifert (1964) at the Toby Jug roundabout. Richard Jefferies, the author and naturalist, lived from 1877 to 1882, at 396 Ewell Road, when fields stretched from here to Ewell.

Tongham [4] An untidy village between Aldershot and the Hog's Back with former hop orchards on the Farnham side, and some

old farms with remnants of oast houses. The church of St Paul is by E. Christian, 1865.

Virginia Water [1] Twentieth-century shopping parade and meaner housing near the station but westwards the lushest residential suburb in the county. The two-mile-long lake of Virginia Water within Windsor Great Park was created in 1746–68 by the artist brothers Thomas and Paul Sandby for "Butcher" Cumberland. Christ Church is 13th-century Gothic of 1831 by W. F. Pocock. N of the station is Holloway Sanatorium, completed in 1884 as another colossal munificence by Thomas Holloway, the pill manufacturer (cf. Egham: Royal Holloway College),

and again designed by W. H. Crossland but in a more Flemish brick and stone Gothic. Towards Sunningdale is Fort Belvedere, a triangular folly tower built for the Duke of Cumberland in 1750 (housing his collection of cannons), but converted by Wyatville in 1827–29 into a dwelling for George IV. It was the favourite private residence of the Duke of Windsor from 1930 until his abdication in 1936.

Wallington* [6] An old established manufacturing town on the Wandle with a large London dormitory area spreading S to downland where it is bisected by the Brighton motorway. In London Road near the river are a few old houses and in Woodcote Road

173

is the Town Hall, a pretty brick and stone building with a central turret by Robert Atkinson, 1935, and opposite a neat new shopping square by R. J. Wood (1965), Holy Trinity Church is by Habershon and Brock (1967), St Elphege's (RC) by Williams and Winkley (1973).

Walton-on-the-Hill [5] The origins of Epsom races on "Walton Downs" are almost forgotten in this suburban village high on the chalk, now better known for the golf-course to its S than the racing stables that survive in pleasant valleys to the NW. The church of St Peter, like much else in the village, was sadly altered in the 19th century. The chancel is 15th century with good Perpendicular details particularly in the chancel. The nave and the W tower are by D. Alexander, 1818. The N aisle was added in 1870 and the upper stages of the tower were rebuilt in 1895. It has a remarkable Romanesque mid-12th-century lead font. It is about 20 inches in diameter, and decorated with bands of foliage and eight figures seated under an arcade of round-headed arches. It was made of one long strip of lead which has been cut down and probably included the 12 apostles. In the SE window of the nave are fragments of English and Flemish stained glass, part local and part brought from Woburn Abbey. NW of the church is Walton Manor, largely of 1891, embedding walls of the hall and chapel of the 14th-century manor house which was for a time the home of Anne of

◁ **Walton-on-the-Hill**: the font

Tilford Bridge

Cleves. In the grounds are the remains of a Norman motte, and another rarity, a well-designed bungalow. S of the church, in the area of expensive houses towards the golf-course, are two by E. Lutyens: Dormy House, 1906, and Chussex, 1908.

Walton-on-Thames [2] A determinedly cheerful town with some good new buildings and a nice stretch of the Thames in an extensive and varied residential area between the river and Painshill (Cobham). St George's Hill, one of the most expensive residential districts in the county, lies within the parish of Walton but is usually thought of as part of Weybridge. The old centre is set back from the river, whose frontage has been spoilt by the invasion of shacks and the ugliest bridge over the Thames. The erection of tower blocks of flats and the creation of the new shopping area on New Zealand Avenue, which is as brash as anything around London (by R. Seifert, 1965), destroyed its former villagey character. Its vulgarity was given an official seal of approval by the U.D.C.'s offices in 1965. NE of this and almost hidden is the fine late 15th-century timber-framed Old Manor House, once the home of John Bradshaw, the Parliamentarian (1602–59). Another great Parliamentarian, Henry Ireton (1611–51), lived at 47 High Street. Of the church of St Mary, the principal historic building in Walton, the N arcade has late Norman circular piers, with scalloped circular capitals. Most of the rest is early 14th century. In the N aisle is a monument of national importance, to Richard Boyle, Viscount Shannon (d 1740), by Roubiliac (1755) representing the Viscount standing in front of a gun and large tent with his daughter ("justly sensible of the inexpressible loss of

her respectable parents") leaning on an urn below. Near it are some 16th-century brasses, one showing John Selwyn, keeper of Oatlands Park (d 1587), killing a stag at the feet of Queen Elizabeth I, a relief by Chantrey commemorating Mr and Mrs C. D'Oyly (1821) and a slab to Wm Lilly, the astrologer who died at Hersham in 1681 and is buried here. Near the station are the large Bird's Eye Foods offices of three storeys with symmetrical elevations in rhythmic-patterned concrete frames by Sir John Burnet, Tait and Partners (1962), well landscaped by P. Hicks, while in King's Road is the swimming pool by Arup Associates. It has a great glazed wall looking over a park, and is dark panelled outside and delicately light inside (1965).

To the west in Oatlands Road are two small estates by Eric Lyons. The best is Templemere (1964) where polygonal two-storey houses are grouped between mature trees saved from older gardens, the best lesson in acceptable redevelopment at higher densities to be found in the County. Upstream from the Bridge were the Cowey Stakes, where Julius Caesar's army is supposed to have forded the Thames in his second invasion of Britain.

Wanborough [4] A manor house, farm barns, and chapel in a group of trees on the otherwise bare northern slope of the Hog's Back. The tiny church of St Bartholomew is a single-roomed 13th-century building with flint walls, in ruins by the 17th century and restored in 1861–2. The Manor is a three-storeyed, three-gabled, half-H, house dated 1527 but largely refronted in the 17th century.

Warlingham* [6] A London dormitory on high downland at the SE end of London sprawl but with less character or independ-

ence than many places nearer the City. It is scenically better in the deep hillsides towards Caterham where lush trees hide the houses. The old village is centred on two small triangular greens, with bottle-brushed trees. The church is north of the greens. Church and street look villagey at a distance but dull on closer inspection. All Saints has 13th-century aisleless nave and chancel with no chancel arch and a S aisle added by P. M. Johnston in 1893. The NE window in the nave has some 15th-century glass, a 15th-century font ornamented with a grotesque head, two sets of piscinae and sedilia on the S side, another piscina on the N, and remains of a big 15th-century wall painting of St Christopher carrying Christ. The English Prayer Book was given its first reading in this church in 1549. Other buildings of interest are the Old White Lion on the northern green, part flint and brick and part tilehung, the plain Attwood almshouses in Leas Road of 1663 with two-storey cottages centres and single-storey wings, and the old Vicarage in Westhall Road, a 17th-century pilastered brick building.

Waverley [7] In a Wey valley meadow E of Farnham, sheltered by the elbow of pine-clad hills around Crooksbury, are the remains of Waverley Abbey, the first house of the Cistercian Order in England. Founded in 1128 its first church was completed by mid-century. After flood damage a second was built in a severe 13th-century style N of the first. The Abbey was never rich and was dissolved under the Act for monastic reform of 1536. The remains, of Burgate stone with creamy Reigate and clunch stone dressings, are simple. Uncluttered, charming but not very informative fragments of the S transepts of the great

The Boyle monument, **Walton-on-Thames** ▷

church, which was 322 feet in length, an end wall of the Monk's Dorter with three lancets, and much of the Cellarium, are all of the 13th century. Across a lake from the ruins is the large house called Waverley, an early 19th-century rebuilding of an 18th-century house by Colin Campbell. Sir Walter Scott was much taken by the ruins and their setting and named his "Waverley" novels after them. On the Elstead Road, across the Wey to the NW is Moor Park, a white house with 18th-century exterior encasing the early 17th-century house purchased in 1680 by Sir William Temple, who renamed it after the Hertfordshire house whose gardens he admired. Here Jonathan Swift was employed as secretary to Sir William and met Esther Johnson, "Stella" of his Journal. Inside, some of the later 18th-century decoration, such as Cundy's work on the staircase, is still attractive. Neglected gardens near the river were part of the history of English landscape gardening, for they were built to exemplify Temple's ideas for more informal picturesque gardening than the French practice then common. Stella's Cottage still stands on the bridge between Waverley and Moor Park.

Westcott [5] A village of Dorking made deliberately picturesque by Victorians and then ordinary by 20th-century commuters. The centre is a triangular green, known to travellers on A25, while the parish church of Holy Trinity by G. G. Scott (1852) is offset on Westcott Common to the W. Pleasant older houses are scattered

(*below and opposite*) **Waverley Abbey**

about, mainly N of the green, and good early Victorian houses infilled round the green and along the Dorking road. To the W are the 16th-century Churtgate House on Guildford Road and 17th-century Rookery Farm in Balchin's Lane. In "The Rookery" (now demolished), ¾ mile W of the green, Thomas Malthus was born in 1766, and here he wrote his "Essay on the Principle of Population" (1798).

Westhumble [5] A few houses in the Vale near Box Hill Station, unfortunately expanded into a dormitory suburb of London in the 1930s. Houses here painted white catch the eye from Box Hill like waste paper in this lovely valley. There are a few neater, better houses in the grounds of the former Camilla Lacey, the home Fanny Burney built with the profits of her novels.

Weybourne [4] A hamlet north of Farnham almost over-run by Aldershot. Only the Old House, a brick building with Baroque elevations dated 1724, is of interest.

Weybridge [5] A medieval village like Walton, shy of the Thames, converted into a gigantic London suburb. It has little unity and no good centre but its suburban fringes such as Oatlands and St George's Hill are some of the most handsome residential areas in the Home Counties. The High Street has survived invasion of the multiple stores and still looks villagey. The parish church is near its W end towards the river Wey, which joins the Thames here. St James was entirely rebuilt by J. L. Pearson in 1848 in a thin Decorated style, with a large broach spire added 1855, which is a landmark seen across Wey meadows. The interior has a richly marbled chancel and under the W tower

monuments from the medieval church which include three brasses and 18th- and early 19th-century tablets including one by Chantrey to Frederica, Duchess of York (d 1820).

The other principal church is St Michael's in Grange Road SE of the town centre by Wm Butterfield (1874) in many-coloured bricks with a bellcote. At the E end of High Street facing Monument Green is the 17th-century (and later) Ship Hotel and the York Column, which stood at Seven Dials in London until 1773 and was re-erected on the Green in 1822 as a memorial to the Duchess of York, who lived at Oatlands. Oatlands Park to the NE was the site of a palace built in 1588 for Henry VIII and popular with Elizabeth I and later monarchs. Its parkland still surrounds the hotel, which is E of the Palace on the site of a hunting lodge, and there is a Tudor arch and garden wall in Thames Street. The lodge was built by Henry Holland in 1794, converted in 1827 into a private mansion and in 1856 altered to form the present Italianate hotel. The gate piers are by Holland. There was a world-famous 18th-century, two-storeyed, grotto here until 1948. The Brooklands motor racing circuit, first in the country, lies broken under the B.A.C. factory to the S.

Wimbledon* [2] A village engulfed in gigantic dull suburbs internationally known for the annual tournament of the All England Tennis Club. There is a historical museum near the Common, but casual vistors will see few signs of its history for its greatest monument, Wimbledon House, built by Thomas Cecil, first Earl of Exeter, went after World War II and most of Wimbledon looks a prosperous 19th- and 20th-century suburb of London.

The old village is a mile N of the gloomy surroundings of the railway, on a hill-top E of the great Common which with Putney Heath covers 1200 acres. The Common is a gravelly plateau overworn in parts and cut up by golf-club fencing. From 1860 competitions of the National Rifle Association were held here, until they moved to the wider spaces of Bisley in 1890. On the golf-course is Caesar's Camp, an Iron Age hill fort badly injured by a 19th-century speculator and to the N is the windmill, rebuilt 1817, restored 1954, in which Lord Baden-Powell wrote most of *Scouting for Boys* in 1908.

The church of St Mary is in Church Road on the ridge east of the Common, where its spired tower is a prominent landmark. It was rebuilt in 1788 and again in 1843 (by G. G. Scott) and the chancel was further altered by Scott in 1860. It is now of flint with stone dressings and has Perpendicular details to match the early 17th-century Cecil chapel S of the chancel. The latter is of brick with a ribbed vault and houses the simple black marble monument over the tomb of Sir Edward Cecil, Viscount Wimbledon (of 1638). The chapel windows contain a late 14th-century figure of St George and 17th-century armorial bearings of the Cecils. A war memorial chapel by T. G. Jackson was added in 1921. To the NW is the Old Rectory, of about 1500 with many additions and alterations, in which Sir Thomas Cecil lived before the completion of his mansion. The mansion itself was E of the church and part of its grounds, landscaped by L. Brown with a lake and fine trees, are preserved as an open space by the Corporation. 17th- and 18th-century Wimbledon spread along the S side and part of the W side of the Common.

Woking Mosque

The most important old house is now Eagle House in High Street, a three-storeyed, three-gabled house of 1613 built in brick but rendered over by T. G. Jackson, the architect, who lived there. It was used as a school for some years, where Schopenhauer was a pupil in 1803. On the S side of the Common is King's College School, founded in 1829 and moved here in 1897. The buildings include a house of 1750 and a main range of Perpendicular style buildings by the architect-historian Banister Fletcher, 1899. Charles Kingsley and D. G. Rossetti were pupils when the school was still in the Strand. Thomas Hughes wrote *Tom Brown's School-days* at the Firs in Ridgeway nearby where he lived from 1853–9. In Spencer Hill, back towards the station, is the red brick St John's church by T. G. Jackson, 1875. Further W is the stone Christ Church by S. S. Teulon, 1860. West Side runs N from the end of South Side and has Georgian but much-altered houses, *e.g.* West Side House of 1750, Cannizaro House rebuilt after a fire in 1899 in a heavy neo-Georgian—but retaining its delightful gardens at the rear, Stamford House of 1720 and the early 19th-century The Kier with a Grecian porch.

The All England Tennis Club, whose first tournament was held in 1877, moved in 1922 to N end of Church Road.

The Town Hall, near the station, and the only building of importance S of the railway, is by Bradshaw, Gass and Hope, 1931.

Windlesham [4] Close knotted small suburbs and intense nursery gardens on Bagshot sands. The church and rectory stand apart, in better but still light farmland. St John the Baptist, burnt in 1680 and rebuilt in brick with stone quoins, was altered by the additions of a tower by Robert Ebbels in 1838 and then swamped by a new nave and N aisle in rather harsh many-coloured bricks by Ewan Christian in 1874. The S side retains late 17th-century brick work and 17th-century porch as well as two Decorated and one Perpendicular window saved from the medieval church. This and the adjoining early 18th-century brick house, The Cedars, make an attractive picture. There are few good houses of any date in the area but in Pound Lane is the attractive 17th-century timber-framed Pound Cottage with gigantic thatched roof (rare in Surrey) sweeping down on each side, with some Regency details facing the garden.

Wisley [5] Mostly a sandy common on the Portsmouth Road and adjoining Gardens of the Royal Horticultural Society. Church and Church Farm are isolated in damp meadows by the Wey to the N and a small hamlet along the lane winding S to the gardens is now largely an estate village of the R.H.S. The church is largely 12th century, much restored, with shingled bell-turret and small spire. A 17th-century porch shelters a restored Norman door. The farmhouse is 17th century and later, L-shaped, half-timbered with red brick infilling. The nucleus of the Gardens, purchased in 1904 and much expanded later to provide for research and extensive plant trials, was that of a pioneer Surrey gardener, G. F. Wilson, Treasurer of the R.H.S., who constructed one of the first "wild" gardens in the world here from 1878 on, full of newly introduced plants.

Witley [7] A village of low half-timber, brick and tilehung cottages stretching S from Milford along the Midhurst Road. It became popular with Victorian artists and writers, who made the place more picturesque, and then with 20th-century commuters, who built great suburban additions to the W, luckily out of sight from the principal road. The best group of buildings is around the church. All Saints has a crossing tower and octagonal shingled spire—the picturesque focus of the building group. The large nave is part of the original Saxon church, extended by the Normans and its original E end can be seen on the S side of the crossing. The roughly carved S doorway is late 11th century. The S transept and chancel were added at the end of the 12th century, the N chapel in the 13th, and the N transept and N aisles in the latter part of the 19th. The chancel, decorated with Victorian stencilling and marble, retains a 13th-century piscina with aumbry above (a position not otherwise found in Surrey). The octagonal Purbeck marble, 13th-century font has octagonal stem and eight shafts merging into one capital. Faded early 12th-century wall paintings on the nave S wall illustrate the life of the Virgin. The N chapel has a brass dated 1525, and heraldic stained glass of the 15th century. The 15th- and 16th-century Old Cottage and Step Cottage, timber-framed with painted brick infill below, the upper storeys oversailing, part tilehung, part weatherboarded, are the picturesque neighbours of the church. In the street are many other timber-framed and brick-filled cottages.

At Wormley, which joins Witley on the south are the buildings of King Edward's school, a dull neo-Jacobean work of Sidney Smirke with plain additions of the 1960's by G. D. Sykes, while one mile further S is Tigbourne Court, a delightful house, perhaps the best work of E. Lutyens, built in

1899, of Burgate stone cut to imitate bricks (a fashion common in 18th-century West Surrey) with tiled roof. The body is of three storeys, but the entrance front is U-shaped with single-storey wings coming forward to end in great coupled chimneys flanked by curved screen walls. It is beautifully textured with galleting around the Burgate stone, and horizontal bands of brick and tiles which gently pull the house and wings together. The landscape painter Myles Birket Foster (d 1897) did the greater part of his work in this village, and George Eliot wrote her last novel, "Daniel Deronda", at her holiday home, The Heights, in 1874–6.

For Witley Park *see* Brook.

Woking [4] New Woking is an invention of the railway, for when the London–Southampton railway arrived here in 1838 there was only bare heath and a pub; the village of Old Woking was a barren mile and a half away. Old Woking is still there, much battered, while the heath in all directions from the station is covered with 19th- and 20th-century houses, pine trees and shrubs. It is pleasant enough outside the dismal grid of mid-19th-century streets and mean shops in the centre. The new shop and office complex by Scott, Brownrigg and Turner and civic buildings by Gollins, Melvin and Ward (1974) will give it a fresh start. The churches are also mean, although the largest, Christ Church, by W. F. Unsworth (1899) is good simple lancet brick. There is also the toylike Shah Jehan Mosque in Oriental Road, which is in an Indian style with onion dome and delicate N front in blue and gold mosaic, designed by W. I. Chambers (1899).

The rest of Woking is noted for its nursery gardens which flourish on the light soil but are being driven slowly out by new housing. Westwards on the Smarts Heath ridge is an estate developed by the London Necropolis Company on land surplus to their giant cemetery at Brookwood, which has two Lutyens houses, Fisher's Hill in neo-Tudor brick (1900) and the simpler Fisher's Hill Cottage.

Old Woking is a badly treated main street with mixed industry and shopping and one corner, near the old church, not hideously ruined. St Peter's is between tall 18th-century houses and the river Wey at the end of Church Street, S of the main road. Due to the building of churches in newer Woking it has been spared the restorations and additions of most Surrey churches and retains a medieval atmosphere. It is entered under the 13th–15th century W tower, by way of a Norman doorway with contemporary metal straps and hinges on its timber door. The nave walls are Norman, the chancel is 13th century, the S aisle and its arcade are 15th century and outside is a low late-Tudor porch, now blocked. The interior contains an ornamental W gallery, dated 1622, presented by Sir Edward Zouch in 1622, a pulpit of the same period, and two 16th-century brasses.

NE is the much-altered 17th-century Hoe Place with an early 18th-century staircase painted by Verrio, and another mile E, beyond Woking's sewage works and hidden in meadows by the willow-fringed Wey, are the slight remains of Woking Old Hall, a minor Tudor palace. This was given by James I to Edward Zouch, who rebuilt at Hoe Place rather than in these damp meadows. Remains are parts of the double moat by the Wey, a long length of Tudor walling with a gateway, and some foundations. Associated relics can be found in the 17th-century brickwork of buildings at Woking Park Farm, and the Old House on Old Woking Road.

See also Sutton Place

Woldingham [6] A well-treed island of development in high chalk downland, saved from self-destruction by Green Belt restrictions. The disused church of St Agatha is the smallest in Surrey, rebuilt in flint in 1832 and, with fittings removed, of little interest in or out. The new church of St Paul, about half a mile further N was built in 1933 by Sir Herbert Baker in a neat Perpendicular style in flint, as a memorial to the shipowner Lord Inchcape (d 1932). The expressionist stained-glass windows in the chancel are by Douglas Strachan. There is one good modern bungalow in Lunghurst Road by Derek Lovejoy (1960), where the pretty hillside setting appears to flow right through the house.

Wonersh [8] A sinuous street of sandstone, brick, half-timber and tilehung buildings leading from Bramley to a tiny triangular "place", and then opening northwards onto a sinuous green towards Shalford, all overlooked by the conical hill of Chinthurst. The church of St John the Baptist, at the Bramley end of the village, has fragments of pre-Conquest date (N wall of nave), also of the 12th and 13th centuries and a simple classical tower of 1751. It was all rebuilt in 1793 after a fire. The nave was then extended over the width of the former S aisle leaving the chancel off-centre, but this was partly remedied by Sir Charles Nicholson who rebuilt the E end, adding a chancel screen. The mainly blue- and red-stained glass window at the E end is the first work (1914) of Sir Charles' brother Archibald. There are

earlier stained-glass armorial bearings on the S side windows, a late 14th-century table tomb in the N chapel and two brasses of 1467 and 1503 in the chancel. Of Wonersh Park, the 17th-century mansion which adjoined, only the 18th-century Gothic gateway on the road and 18th-century stables, made into dwellings, remain. One of Lutyens' earliest houses is on the village side of Chinthurst Hill, built 1893 in a Tudor style of Burgate stone cut to imitate bricks. Great Tangley Manor, the most impressive half-timbered house in

◁ **Merrist Wood, Worplesdon**

the county, lies in a moat N of the common. Dated 1584 it has been much altered and extended. The main front is three gabled, each with unequal oriel windows and a double overhang, and has curved braces producing patterns of star shapes and circles intersecting square panel frames more common to W Midland counties. There are simple panelled interiors and contemporary overmantels. The W and E ends are by Philip Webb.

Worplesdon [4] Round a sinuous green between barren common to the E and improved farmland to

the W it is pleasantly villagey in spite of its easy access to Guildford, Woking and London, and since its setting is undulating either the strong Perpendicular tower of St Mary or the ridge of the Hog's Back to the S gives interest to its views. The church is E of the green. The N chapel is 13th century, "restored" in 1866, while the nave, two aisles and W tower were built or enlarged in the 15th century. The imposing tower contains a five light W window and is nicely capped by a cupola from the rectory stables, put here in 1766. The E window of the N aisle has the two best 14th-century stained-

The Tortoise House, Wotton

glass figures in the county, in reds and green under elaborate canopies. The late 17th-century marble font and 17th-century pulpit were brought from Eton College. Of the number of old houses in the village and around it, the best are two 17th-century timber-fronted farmhouses, Pitch Place (formerly Cobbetts and dated 1683), and Norton Farm NW of the village while Littlefield Manor towards Wood Street has an ornamental brick front of the late 17th century. Merrist Wood, to the W, now an Agricultural College, is one of Norman Shaw's best houses. Part half-timbered, part Burgate stone, built in 1877 on a ridge with a view S over its own well-tended farmland to the Hog's Back.

Wotton [5] Like adjoining Abinger the parish is long and thin, stretching from the wooded crest of the North Downs around Ranmore (qv) S over vale, and Greensand hills to the heavy clay Weald. There is the ancestral home of the Evelyn family near the centre and a church isolated on a little hill facing the Downs, but no real village though estate houses in the damp bottom W of the House are being replaced by new houses on conspicuous ground at the top of Coast Hill, which should have been Green Belt land. St John's is mainly local sandstone with a Horsham slate roof. It has pre-Conquest W tower and chancel, 13th-century nave, N transept and N (or Evelyn) chapel, and outside that the late 17th-century brick mausoleum of the Evelyn family. The tower was once central for an earlier nave stood on its west side. The later S porch shelters a 13th-century doorway adorned with nine tiny, well-carved, heads which represent a pre-reformation quarrel between the English and Roman churches. The interest of the interior is in the Evelyn memorials. The tombs of John Evelyn, the diarist, (d 1706) and his wife (d 1709) are on the N side

Wotton House

St John's **Wotton**

of the N chapel marked by plain coffin-shaped slabs. Those of his grandfather George, the great gunpowder maker (d 1603), with his two wives and of his father Richard (d 1634) and mother have kneeling figures richly adorned but coarse in design and execution. More Evelyn memorials in the Mausoleum include a tablet of 1778 by R. Chambers and another of 1829 by Westmacott. Wotton House, the Evelyn family home since the 16th century, lies ¾ miles SW of the church in the steep valley of the Tillingbourne. The, then Tudor, house was bought by George Evelyn, who came from Thames Ditton,

and died here in 1603. Its best-known owner John Evelyn, his younger grandson, the diarist and arboriculturalist, was born here in 1620, but left at the age of five and came back to live only in 1694.

The house, attractively set in the wooded valley, is a muddle of additions and alterations from Tudor times to the 19th century. Hawksmoor, Kent and Woodyer, as well as many Evelyns, have all left some mark but it is now not even picturesque thanks to Woodyer's hard neo-Tudor facing. It is now leased to the Fire Service College.

Of the historically important gardens laid out for his brother by

John Evelyn from 1643 onwards there remain ponds on the Tillingbourne, a great mound with terrace commanding the S side of the house with a recessed temple at its foot, and the late 18th-century, two-storeyed, "Tortoise Houses", a summer house with open arcades (now in poor condition) facing N to an overgrown formal pool. The Evelyn estate spreads S, past the delectable hamlet of Friday Street (qv), and Broadmoor where the Evelyns made an artificial waterfall on a steep hillside by long diversion of the Tillingbourne through pine-woods to Leith Hill (qv) the highest point in SE England.

189